ROBERT LOUIS STEVENSON
in the South Seas

Portrait of Robert Louis Stevenson

R.L.S.

IN THE SOUTH SEAS

AN INTIMATE PHOTOGRAPHIC RECORD

With an introduction and edited by
ALANNA KNIGHT

MAINSTREAM
PUBLISHING

First published in the United Kingdom by
Mainstream Publishing, Edinburgh.
The publisher acknowledges subsidy from the Scottish Arts Council
towards the publication of this volume.

MAINSTREAM PUBLISHING COMPANY (EDINBURGH), LTD.
7 Albany Street
Edinburgh EH1 3UG

ISBN 1 85158 013 1

Typeset in 12 on 13 Van Dijck by Mainstream Publishing.
Printed by Collins, Glasgow, Great Britain.

DEDICATION

For
Konrad Hopkins
and
David Jensen

Acknowledgements

Photographs (unless otherwise stated) are reproduced by courtesy of the Edinburgh City Libraries, whose invaluable assistance and many kindnesses during the production of this volume are gratefully acknowledged.

Photographs on pages 47-50, 81 and 123 by kind permission of University of Oklahoma.

Literary excerpts:
THE WORKS OF ROBERT LOUIS STEVENSON, Tusitala Edition (Heinemann, London 1924): *In the South Seas*, (Vol. 20); *Vailima Papers* — A Footnote to History; Father Damien, (Vol. 21); *Letters, Volume III* (Vol. 33).
AN INTIMATE PORTRAIT OF R.L.S. by Lloyd Osbourne (Scribner's Magazine, New York, 1924).
THE CRUISE OF THE 'JANET NICOLL' AMONG THE SOUTH SEA ISLANDS by Mrs R. L. Stevenson (Chatto & Windus, London 1915).
FROM SARANAC TO THE MARQUESAS & BEYOND by Mrs Margaret Isabella Balfour Stevenson (Methuen, London, 1903).

Recommended Reading

Day, A. Grove: TRAVELS IN HAWAII (University Press of Hawaii, Honolulu, 1973).

Ferguson, De Lancey & Waingrow, Marshall: ROBERT LOUIS STEVENSON'S LETTERS TO CHARLES BAXTER (Oxford University Press, 1956).

Field, Isobel (Belle Strong): THIS LIFE I'VE LOVED (Michael Joseph, London, 1937).

Fletcher, C. Brundson: STEVENSON'S GERMANY: THE CASE AGAINST GERMANY IN THE PACIFIC (Heinemann, London, 1920).

Furnas, J. C: VOYAGE TO WINDWARD (Faber & Faber, London 1952).

Knight, Alanna: ROBERT LOUIS STEVENSON TREASURY (Shepheard-Walwyn, London, 1985).

McGaw, Sister Martha Mary: STEVENSON IN HAWAII (University of Hawaii Press, Honolulu 1950).

Mackay, Margaret: THE VIOLENT FRIEND: THE STORY OF MRS ROBERT LOUIS STEVENSON (Doubleday, New York 1968: Dent, London 1969).

Menikoff, Barry: R.L.S. & THE BEACH OF FALESA (Edinburgh University Press 1984).

Mrantz, Maxine: R. L. STEVENSON: POET IN PARADISE (Aloha Graphics, Honolulu, 1977).

Stevenson, Fanny Van der Grift & Robert Louis: OUR SAMOAN ADVENTURE, Weidenfeld & Nicholson, London 1956.

Author's Note

The original text (Tusitala Edition 1924) has been used for Stevenson's letters. There are some irregularities in spelling; also 'Taiti' becomes the conventional 'Tahiti' in later letters. Fanny used 'Nichol' instead of 'Nicoll' (correct) in her Diary of the cruise. The elipses in letters most frequently indicate a repetition in other letters or in Margaret Stevenson's letters to her sister, where the same event was being described by both writers, or when Stevenson's letters were dealing with business or writing projects at some length.

Regarding Stevenson's main correspondents: Charles Baxter (1848-1919) was an Edinburgh Lawyer, a friend since student days and in charge of his affairs while abroad. Sir Sidney Colvin (1845-1927) had been introduced to Stevenson by Fanny Sitwell (later to become Lady Colvin) during the time of Stevenson's infatuation for this 'older woman' in 1873. The friendship with novelist Henry James (1843-1916) dates from Bournemouth days (1885); also with Adelaide Boodle, a neighbour at 'Skerryvore' who became a devoted friend.

Fanny, Belle Strong, Louis and Mrs Margaret Stevenson

Contents

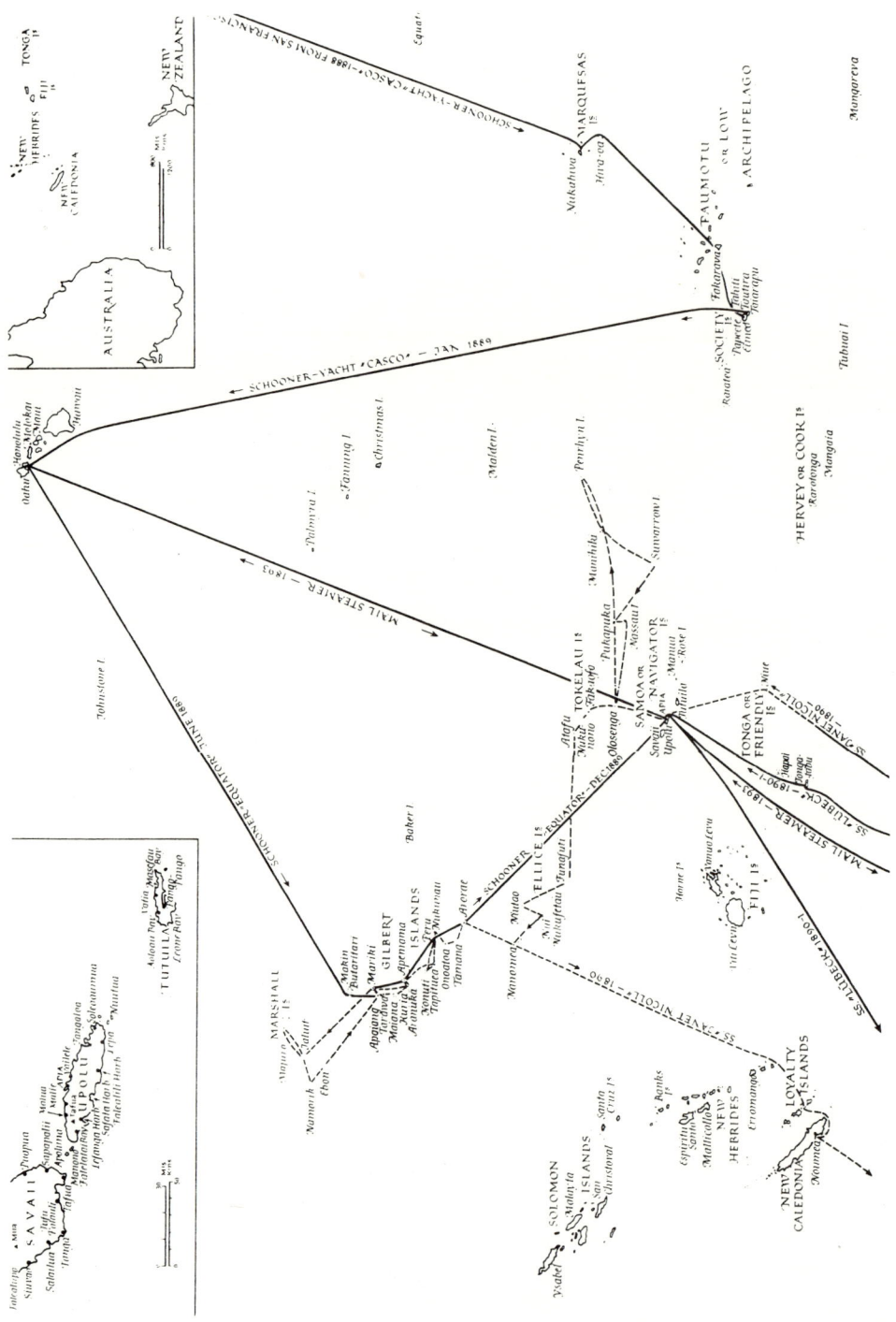

Map of Stevenson's 3 Cruises

List of Illustrations

INTRODUCTION

In 1879 Robert Louis Stevenson first visited America, his main purpose to marry Fanny Osbourne. At that time he was twenty-nine years old and a relatively unknown Scottish writer. Eight years later, in 1887, New York gave a hero's welcome to 'R.L.S.', the famous author of *Dr Jekyll and Mr Hyde* and *Kidnapped*, who was then a chronic invalid returning to America in search of health.

During a winter of appalling severity in Saranac, New York State, Stevenson supported his family by writing articles for the New York *World*. Its editor, Sam McClure, suggested chartering a yacht to voyage in the South Seas, to be financed by a syndicated weekly column, with payment guaranteed beforehand. Stevenson responded with enthusiasm. Long before his success with *Treasure Island* (1882), a New Zealand visitor to his Edinburgh home had told him:

> . . . all about the South Sea Islands till I was sick with desire to go there; beautiful places, green for ever; perfect climate, perfect shapes of men and women with red flowers in their hair; and nothing to do but study oratory and etiquette, sit in the sun and pick up the fruits as they fall. Navigator's Island is the place; absolute balm for the weary.

A chance remark to Fanny, who was visiting her family in California, led to her chartering the schooner-yacht *Casco*, a ninety-five-feet schooner, seventy-two tons register, the property of a wealthy doctor. The *Casco*, with a crew of eleven, set sail under the command of Captain A. H. Otis. The captain was unimpressed by his distinguished passenger, having read *Treasure Island* and having dismissed it as an example of poor seamanship.

Stevenson wrote few letters after the first voyage. His mother, Margaret Stevenson, writing to her sister, Jane Whyte Balfour in Edinburgh, in a letter reproduced in *From Saranac to the Marquesas* (1903), provides a vivid account of everyday life on an ocean-going yacht. There was a reason:

> By the way, Louis would like you to keep all the letters I write on the voyage for his benefit, as he may want to refer to them if ever he brings out a book. . . .

The health-seeking cruise of a few months' duration now held the exciting prospect of a definitive illustrated history of the South Seas and for this more ambitious project their luggage included a typewriter, cameras, photographic equipment and a magic lantern.

Photography at this time was a novel but very haphazard hobby for amateurs. The photographic camera had developed from the camera obscura, familiar to artists and scientists since the seventeenth century as a portable drawing instrument, complete with lens and focusing mechanism. Had the science of chemistry been as far advanced as optics, then photography would have been in use much earlier.

In 1816, a Frenchman, Joseph Nicéphore Niépce, had substituted paper, light-sensitised with silver salts, for ground glass but was unable to print positive impressions from his negatives. Niépce's introduction of bellows and iris diaphragm was a great step forward, and in 1830 another Frenchman, J. M. Daguerre, used similar camera obscuras fitted with an achromatic meniscus lens. This become known as the daguerreotype process. The first commercially available camera was made by his brother-in-law, Alphonse Giroux, for Daguerre in 1839, but like Niépce's model it was bulky and consisted of two wooden boxes of similar size to produce wholeplate pictures, with a lens cap to act as shutter.

William Henry Fox-Talbot had also experimented in 1834-35 with the camera obscura, but for large objects and buildings this process took hours to gather enough darkening to form an image. By accident, he discovered the process of development which, with the action of gallic acid, multiplied the silver grains.

Further progress was made in 1851 by Frederick Scott Archer's discovery of coating glass plates with collodion. Wet collodion photographs opened up a new dimension but the main drawback was that photographers had to carry a portable darkroom to operate the process. For outdoor work such cumbersome equipment was inconvenient, even though ambitious projects such as Roger Fenton's Crimean War photographs were made possible. Before wet collodion, it had been practically impossible to capture movement, and sitters had to be 'clamped' in place; however, this process reduced exposure times from minutes to seconds or tenths of seconds. It opened up a new era of photography. Scott Archer did not apply for a patent and, as no licence was required, anyone able to afford the equipment could set himself up in business. At the same time, public interest in photography was increasing: family groups were greatly in demand, and even Queen Victoria had her own darkroom specially equipped in Windsor Castle.

In 1875 the first book of photo journalism, *Street Life in London*, was published. Tripods and camera with collapsible bellows became available and, in 1881, Kodak introduced their first camera. George Eastmann replaced glass with flexible celluloid and in 1885 a simple box camera containing a 100-exposure roll film followed. Ten years later, in 1895 (the year after Stevenson's death in Samoa), the first 'pocket Kodak' was on the market.

The period of Stevenson's voyages — 1888-1890 — therefore, covers the rapid development of portable photography. There is no indication in the letters from the voyages of the models used, but we can presume from Margaret Stevenson's references to 'field' camera, plate films and the exhausting carrying of heavy equipment and tripod that roll films were either still too novel or too expensive to

Lloyd Osbourne, Fanny and Louis Stevenson at Saranac

be in general use. Writing to Charles Baxter from Tahiti, Stevenson apologises for 'bad proofs' because 'the paper was so bad'.

While his stepson, Lloyd Osbourne, is often referred to as 'taking pictures', one Stevenson letter suggests that using the camera was an entire family activity: 'We are all pretty gay on board, and have been photographing and draught-playing and skylarking like anything.' We know also that Stevenson, travelling alone to the leper settlement, took his camera.

There are almost ninety photographs in this book. There should have been twice that number. Fanny Stevenson's diary, *The Cruise of the "Janet Nicol" Among the South Sea Islands*, records that ninety were lost in a disastrous shipboard fire in April 1890, doubtless including those Stevenson intended sending to Burlingame, his editor, at Scribner's:

> . . . a portrait of Tembinoka, a view of the palace or of some of the 'matted men' at their singing, also T's flag, which my wife designed for him, and a few photographs of the war, which will do for illustrations [for the projected travel book].

In a letter from Anaho Bay, 29 July 1889, Margaret Stevenson also recounts other disasters, in particular:

> Today a great misfortune has befallen us; Lloyd's camera has fallen overboard. It had been left overnight onshore, and was brought out this morning; and while being handed up from the boat, slipped out of its strap and went straight to the bottom. Lloyd has taken a few pictures, but it is a serious loss coming so early in our trip. . . .

Then from Hiva-Oa, on 25 August:

> We got one piece of good news, young Keane has a camera and has used up all his plates, so was quite willing to sell it to Lloyd, who thinks he can cut his plates to fit it.

At sea or on land Stevenson's main preoccupation was the daily exercise of his writing craft. He had no excuse for dallying; he was a good sailor, his health was excellent, and his mother declared his appetite splendid, considering him fitter than at any time in the past ten years. In Tahiti during October 1888 he worked on *The Master of Ballantrae*, to be published in twelve monthly instalments in *Scribner's Magazine* (November 1888-October 1889). To Colvin he wrote: 'it [*The Master of Ballantrae*] contains more human work than anything of mine but *Kidnapped*.'

On arrival at Papeete in Tahiti, Stevenson fell victim to the 'new' island epidemic, influenza. He was welcomed into the household of the chief, Ori a Ori, at Tautira, where he was nursed by Princess Moe. Soon all three were great friends, 'exchanging names'. His enforced stay produced two South Seas ballads: *Feast of Famine*, a Marquesas story, *Song of Rahero* and, for 'Songs of Travels', the nostalgic 'Home no more home to me, whither must I wander?'. It was not until they reached Honolulu, from where the *Casco* was sent back to its owner in San Francisco, that Stevenson wrote Burlingame in January 1889:

> As soon as I am through with *The Master*, I shall finish *The Game of Bluff* — now rechristened *The Wrong Box* [written in collaboration with his stepson Lloyd Osbourne]. This I wish to sell, cash down. It is of course copyright in the States; and I offer it to you for five thousand dollars. Please reply on this by return. Also please tell the typewriter who was so good as to be amused by our follies that I am filled with admiration for his piece of work. I may also be

Stevenson in 1893

> deceived as to the numbers of *The Master* now going, or already gone; but to me they seem
> First Chop, sir, First Chop. I hope I shall pull off that damned ending; but it still depresses
> me; this is your doing, Mr Burlingame; you would have it there and then, and I fear it — I
> fear that ending.

He finished the book in March and in April wrote again:

> I am quite worked out, and this cursed end of *The Master* hangs over me like the arm of the
> gallows; but it is always darkest before dawn and no doubt the clouds will soon rise; but it is a
> difficult thing to write, above all in Mackellarese [the narrator], and I cannot yet see my way
> clear. If I pull this off, *The Master* will be a pretty good novel or I am the more deceived; and
> even if I don't pull it off, it'll still have some stuff in it.'

To Will Low, on 20 May:

> I have at length finished *The Master*; it has been a sore cross to me; but now he is buried, his
> body's under hatches — his soul, if there is any hell to go to, gone to hell; and I forgive him;
> it is harder to forgive Burlingame for having induced me to begin the publication, or myself
> for suffering the induction.

By October he and Lloyd were at work on *The Wrecker*. To Colvin, he wrote:

> ... strange ways of life, I think, they set forth: things I can scarce touch upon, or even not at
> all, in my travel book; and the yarns are good, I do believe. *The Pearl Fisher* [later retitled *The
> Ebb Tide*] is for the *New York Ledger*; the yarn is a kind of Monte Cristo one. *The Wrecker* is the
> least good as a story, I think; but the characters seem to me good. *The Beachcombers* is more
> sentimental. [This book was never written.]

The main task of gathering material for his illustrated history continued and
as early as November 1888 he was optimistically dedicating this work to fellow-
writer John Addington Symonds. In Honolulu the Stevensons made friends with
King Kalakaua, who had a penchant for apeing the manners and methods of
European monarchies, and six months later, in June 1889, they boarded the
Equator, a small copra-trading schooner with a crew of sixteen and a Scottish
captain named Reid, bound for the Gilbert Islands. The Stevensons were to be
dropped at Samoa to take ship to Sydney and, as Stevenson wrote to his mother
(who had returned to Edinburgh to nurse her sister Jane): 'We shall turn up in
England by May or June.' And to Colvin, on 2 December 1889:

> 'I am minded not to stay very long in Samoa and confine my studies there (as far as anyone
> can forecast) to the history of the late war.'

Samoa was first visited by a Dutchman, Jacob Roggeveen, in 1722. The island's
strategic position in the early 1800s combined with its wealth in copra, the oil-
yielding kernel of the coconut, made it an attractive acquisition to Great Britain,
Germany and the United States. In 1878 the three powers signed treaties with the
result that their interests were soon in conflict. The rival factions of Catholic and
Protestant missionaries were also at loggerheads, and the bewildered Samoans
were ruthlessly exploited by the white man, of whom Trader Wiltshire in *The
Beach of Falesá* is a typical example.

In *A Footnote to History*, Stevenson wrote:

> The handful of whites have everything; the natives walk in a foreign town. . . . Within the
> memory of man the white people of Apia lay in the worst squalor of degradation. They are
> now unspeakably improved, both men and women. Today they must be called a more than

'King' Mataafa of Samoa

fairly respectable population, and a much more than fairly intelligent. The trouble (for Samoa) is that they are all here after a livelihood. Some are sharp practitioners, some are famous (justly or unjustly) for foul play in business . . . commerce, like politics shows its ugly side, and becomes as personal as fisticuffs. Close at their elbows, in all this contention, stands the native looking on. Like a child, his true analogue, he observes, apprehends, misapprehends, and is usually silent. . . .

But not all South Sea Islanders were cannibals, nor were all white men corrupt. Harry J. Moors, an American trader and local politician, provides interesting descriptions of Stevenson in *With Stevenson in Samoa*:

A young-looking man came forward to meet me. He appeared to be about thirty years of age, although really nine years older, of fair and somewhat sallow complexion, and about five feet ten inches in height. He wore a slight, scraggy moustache, and his hair hung down about his neck after the fashion of artists. This was Stevenson — R.L.S., 'the best beloved initials in recent literature' — and I knew it even before he spoke. He was not a handsome man, and yet there was something irresistibly attractive about him. The genius that was in him seemed to shine out of his face. I was struck at once by his keen, inquiring eyes, brown in colour they were strangely bright, and seemed to penetrate you like the eyes of a mesmerist. . . . I needed not to be told that he was in indifferent health, for it was stamped on his face. He appeared to be intensely nervous, highly strung, easily excited. When I first brought him ashore he was looking somewhat weak, but hardly had he got into the street when he began to walk up and down it in a most lively, not to say eccentric, manner. He could not stand still. When I took him to my house, he walked about the room, plying me with questions, one after another, darting up and down, talking on all sorts of subjects, with no continuity whatever in his conversation. His wife was just as fidgety as himself, Lloyd Osbourne not much better. The long lonesome trip on the schooner had quite unnerved them, and they were delighted to be on shore again.

Stevenson was very much addicted to the 'bare feet' habit, but before long I became aware of other eccentricities . . . in a rage he was a study. Once excite him, and you had another Stevenson. I have seen him sitting on my table, dangling his bony legs in the air, chatting away in the calmest possible manner; and I have seen him, becoming suddenly agitated, jump from the table and stalk to and fro across the floor like some wild forest animal, to which he has, indeed, been already compared. His face would glow and his eyes would flash, hypnotising you with their brilliance and burning fires within. In calm they were eyes of strange beauty, with an expression that is almost beyond the power of pen to describe. Eyes half alert, half sorrowful, a strange mixture of what seemed to be at once the sorrow and the joy of life, and there appeared to be a haunting sadness in their very brightness.

The Rev. W. E. Clarke, of the London Missionary Society, was less impressed and, at first glimpse, presumed that he was witnessing the arrival of a band of down-at-heel entertainers eager to make a few dollars, while Henry Adams, the American humorist and friend of Henry James, described Stevenson as:

A man so thin and emaciated that he looked like a bundle of sticks in a bag, with dirty striped pyjamas, the baggy legs tucked into coarse woollen stockings, one of which was bright brown in colour, the other a purplish dark tone. . . . He appeared first, looking like an insane stock, very warm and restless.

As for Fanny Stevenson:

A woman in the usual missionary nightgown which was no cleaner than her husband's shirt

Mataafa's rival, Tamasese

and drawers, but she omitted the stockings . . . her complexion and eyes were dark and strong, like a half-breed Mexican. . . .

Moors' account continues:

One day Stevenson told me he would like to make his home in Samoa permanently. 'I like this place better than any I have seen in the Pacific,' he said. Tahiti and the Marquesas pleased him, but of all places he liked Samoa best. 'Honolulu's good — very good,' he added, 'but this seems more savage!' He asked me to look out for a nice piece of property that would suit him. Money matters seemed to trouble him, however — not so much the first cost of the land, but the cost of the improvements that would necessarily have to follow. 'Elbow room! Let's have elbow room!' said Stevenson.

Finally, after several fine properties had been submitted to him for inspection, he decided that the Vailima land was the most attractive. At his request, I negotiated the purchase. There were four hundred acres, and I paid $4000. . . .

During this first sojourn in Samoa, Stevenson completed *The Bottle Imp* before embarking on the third voyage, from Sydney by the steamer *Janet Nicoll*:

. . . near 500 tons, a mighty fine affair for the likes of us; or would be, if she could be induced to stop rolling and wallowing like a drunken tub

wrote Stevenson to his mother, enclosing a plan of accommodation.

The main cabin is 15 feet long, with 7 feet headroom. Above the cabin is a spar deck and above that again the bridge; abaft the cabins are the galley and the engines. It is very pleasant to have the engines behind; but there is no use in trying to blink the fact that the *Janet* is a pig. I never saw such a roller. Again, last night since I began to write, I was nearly thrown out of my bunk, and eating is a toil and trial.

Not surprisingly he was to write later of 'a cruel rough passage to Auckland'. His writing suffered too: *The Wrecker* was in the doldrums.

In August, back in Sydney, he wrote to Marcel Schwob, a Frenchman who wished to translate *The Black Arrow*:

I am just now overloaded with work. I have two huge novels on hand — *The Wrecker* and *The Pearl Fisher* [*The Ebb Tide*] in collaboration with my stepson; the latter, *The Pearl Fisher*, I think highly of, for a black, ugly, trampling, violent story, full of strange scenes and striking characters. And then I am about waist-deep in my big book on the South Seas, *the* big book on the South Seas it ought to be, and shall. And besides, I have some verses in the press, which, however, I hesitate to publish. For I am no judge of my own verse; self-deception is there so facile. All this and cares of an impending settlement in Samoa keep me very busy, and a cold (as usual) keeps me in bed.

Once settled in Samoa, Stevenson's determination to meddle in island politics upset the authorities and caused his friends at home both embarrassment and anxiety. To Sidney Colvin, Stevenson wrote on 9 May 1892:

You are to understand: if I take all this bother, it is not only from a sense of duty, or a love of meddling — damn the phrase, take your choice — but from a great affection for Mataafa. He is a beautiful, sweet old fellow, and he and I grew quite fulsome on Saturday night about our sentiments.

But for the intervention of the British Foreign Secretary, Lord Rosebery, who admired his books, he might well have been deported on the visiting man-of-war lurking in the harbour. Typically, Stevenson immediately made friends with the

Mataafa's natural daughter

crew. Unrepentant, he continued to support the 'rebel' king while his family bore gifts for the lesser chiefs who were imprisoned in Apia. When warriors in war paint, known to take heads, male and female, stared in the windows and the war drums interrupted family prayers, Stevenson would console his terrified womenfolk with a shrug: 'Why worry, we have friends on both sides.' Peace returned to Samoa in 1893 and the chiefs expressed their gratitude by building a link road to Vailima, aptly named 'the Road of Loving Hearts'.

According to Lloyd Osbourne in *An Intimate Portrait*:

> Stevenson made a very large income, and spent it all on Vailima. His letters often show much anxiety about money, and some of his intimate correspondents lectured him severely on his extravagance. Often in moments of depression he called Vailima his Abbotsford, and said he was ruining himself like Scott.

To Colvin on 8 March 1892, Stevenson wrote:

> 'Is this not Babylon the Great I have builded? Call it Subpriorsford.'

Lloyd, Fanny and Louis Stevenson in the Great Hall, Vailima

Dictating to step-daughter Belle in his study

Like Scott, he died of a cerebral haemorrhage from overwork, on 3 December 1894. His life was spartan: sometimes he rose at four a.m. and he wrote at all times and all hours. He described his working day to Colvin (June 1891):

> . . . knee-deep in books, nearly all the shelves are filled, alas. It is a place to make a pig recoil, yet here are my interminable labours begun daily by lamplight and sometimes not yet done when the lamp has once more to be lighted.

Moors quotes his reaction to life in Samoa:

> I love the land; and I have chosen it to be my home while I live, and my grave after I am dead. And I love the people and have chosen them to be my people to live and die with.

And to Colvin, in August 1893, Stevenson wrote:

> I would like you to see Vailima, for it's beautiful and my home and tomb that is to be; though it's a wrench not to be planted in Scotland — that I can never deny — if I could be buried in the hills, under the heather and a table tombstone like the martyrs, where the whaups and plovers are crying. . . . Singular that I should fulfil the Scots destiny throughout, and live a voluntary exile, and have my head filled with the blessed beastly place all the time.

And so it was reflected in his writing in those last years. *Treasure Island* had been written in 1881 during a bleak summer in Scotland, when Stevenson's

On the verandah at Vailima

passion for islands held no hint of the destiny that awaited him. Once settled in Samoa, the short story, *The Beach of Falesá*, was his last work on the South Seas and he proceeded to write out his nostalgia for Scotland with *Catriona, St Ives, Weir of Hermiston*. In place of the 'the *big* book', Stevenson's projected Illustrated History, for which these unique photographs were intended, he completed only *A Footnote to History* and a collection of essays, *In the South Seas*. In conjunction with his *Letters* (from Vol. 3) and extracts from the books above-mentioned, they bring vividly to life Stevenson the writer and champion of lost causes, aboard ship, and at home among the Cannibal Islanders.

Alanna Knight
Aberdeen
April 1986

PART ONE

FIRST VOYAGE
June 1888-January 1889

In the yacht *Casco* for seven months from San Francisco to the Marquesas, the Paumotus, Tahiti, and thence northwards to Hawaii.

Mrs Margaret Stevenson wearing lei

In the South Seas: The Marquesas
An Island Landfall

For nearly ten years my health had been declining; and for some while before I set forth upon my voyage I believed I was come to the afterpiece of life, and had only the nurse and undertaker to expect. It was suggested that I should try the South Seas; and I was not unwilling to visit like a ghost, be carried like a bale, among scenes that had attracted me in youth and health. I chartered accordingly Dr Merrit's schooner, the *Casco*, seventy-four tons register; sailed from San Francisco towards the end of June 1888, visited the eastern islands, and was left early the next year at Honolulu. Hence, lacking courage to return to my old life of the house and sick-room, I set forth to leeward in a trading schooner, the *Equator*, of a little over seventy tons, spent four months among the atolls (low coral islands)

On board the Casco

of the Gilbert group, reached Samoa towards the close of '89. By that time gratitude and habit were beginning to attach me to the islands; I had gained a competency of strength; I had made friends; I had learned new interests; the time of my voyages had passed like days in fairyland; and I decided to remain. I began to prepare these pages at sea, on a third cruise, in the trading steamer *Janet Nicoll*. If more days are granted me, they shall be passed where I have found life most pleasant and man most interesting; the axes of my black boys are already clearing the foundations of my future house; and I must learn to address readers from the uttermost parts of the sea.

Letter from Mrs Margaret Stevenson to Jane Whyte Balfour
Yacht Casco, *Sunday, July 1 1888*

This is our fourth day at sea and all goes well I am thankful to say. Everybody was at lunch today except Fanny; she and Lloyd and Valentine spent most of their time during the first three days in bed, and even the captain did not appear at meals for two days, so that Louis and I had them all by ourselves. I missed only the first breakfast and that was because I had been on deck for two hours and was not able to face red herrings and mutton chops after that.

We were towed out by the *Pelican*. There was a heavy swell outside and we were amused to watch the little steamer first lifted high above us, and then, as the wave passed, she, and even the mountains of the coast, were shut out entirely. Our vessel seemed very small among those enormous waves, and I felt nervous when I saw how she heeled over; however, I was told it was all right, and I am already getting accustomed to it. The swell, too, is beginning to go down.

I must try to describe the vessel that is to be our home for so long. From the deck you step down into the cockpit, which is our open-air drawing-room. It has seats all round, nicely cushioned, and we sit or lie there most of the day. The compass is there, and the wheel, so the man at the wheel always keeps us company. Here, also, is the companion, and at the bottom of the stair on the right-hand side is the captain's room. Straight ahead is the main or after cabin, a nice bright place with a skylight and four portholes. There are four sofas that can be turned into beds if need be, and there are lockers under them in which our clothes are stored away. Above and behind each sofa is a berth concealed by white lace curtains on brass rods, and in these berths we three women are laid away as on shelves each night to sleep. There is a table fastened to the floor in the centre of the cabin, covered with crimson Utrecht velvet. The sofas are upholstered to match, and the carpet is crimson Brussels. There is one large, heavy swivel chair, and opposite the entrance is a mirror let into the wall, with two small shelves under it. On each side of this mirror is a door. The one to the right leads through a small dressing-room with a fixed basin to Lloyd's cabin, and beyond that again is the forward cabin, or dining-room. The door to the left opens into another small dressing-room, and beyond this is Louis's sleeping-room. It is very roomy, with both a bed and a sofa in it, so that he will be very comfortable; and at night, when we are all in bed, all the portholes and skylights and doors are left open for the sake of air.

The dining-room has a long table and chairs, two mirrors at the end, and between the doors a very ugly picture of fruits and cake. Louis would fain cover it up if we could spare a flag with which to do it. Two doors at the further end lead to the pantry and galley, and beyond these are the men's quarters, which I have not yet explored.

Tuesday, July 3

Sunday was cloudy and squally, but Louis was able to read a short service in the cockpit at 4 p.m., which was the time that suited best for the men. . . . We are nearing the tropics and beginning to feel it. We saw one whale the day we sailed, and four pilot-birds have followed us all the way. It is delightful to see them alighting on the waves and walking along for a few steps, leaving little white foot-prints behind them on the water. Louis says that they follow the vessel for 'grease', and that they suppose the yacht is an immense bird, and that we are the fleas upon its back! . . .

Thursday, July 5

Yesterday we had a new sensation — a calm. The sails flapped idly, and we only made about two knots an hour; the sun was very hot, but we could generally find shade behind one or other of the sails. The sea was beautifully smooth, and we had the rare pleasure of a distant horizon. Usually we seem to be shut in by the waves.

We all had a very active fit. Fanny, Valentine and I took to making pyjamas and jackets for Louis of thin flannel, to be ready for the hot weather. . . . During the day I had a good long walk outside of the cockpit, which was quite a treat. Louis won't let me attempt it unless the sea is very smooth, because the passage is narrow and the bulwarks not very high. He and Fanny think me much too adventurous, and declare I will fall over. Fanny said to the captain one day, 'What would you do if Mrs Stevenson were to fall overboard?' and the captain, who loves a joke, solemnly replied, 'Put it in the log!'. This morning Valentine tossed Fanny's cushion up the companion stairs and very nearly sent it overboard. Louis asked, 'Would you have put that in the log if it had gone over?' 'Yes, if you thought it worth while to send Valentine after it. . . .'
[*Valentine Roch, the Stevensons' Swiss maid*]

July 15

. . . We have had some very hot weather since I last wrote. The thermometer has been up to eighty-nine degrees in the cabin, but is more often about seventy-four degrees, and of course it is hotter on deck. Fanny and Valentine have taken to *mumus* and *holakus* but I am putting off as long as I can. So far I have been content to discard all woollen garments and stiff or fitted bodices, and I often wear boots ·

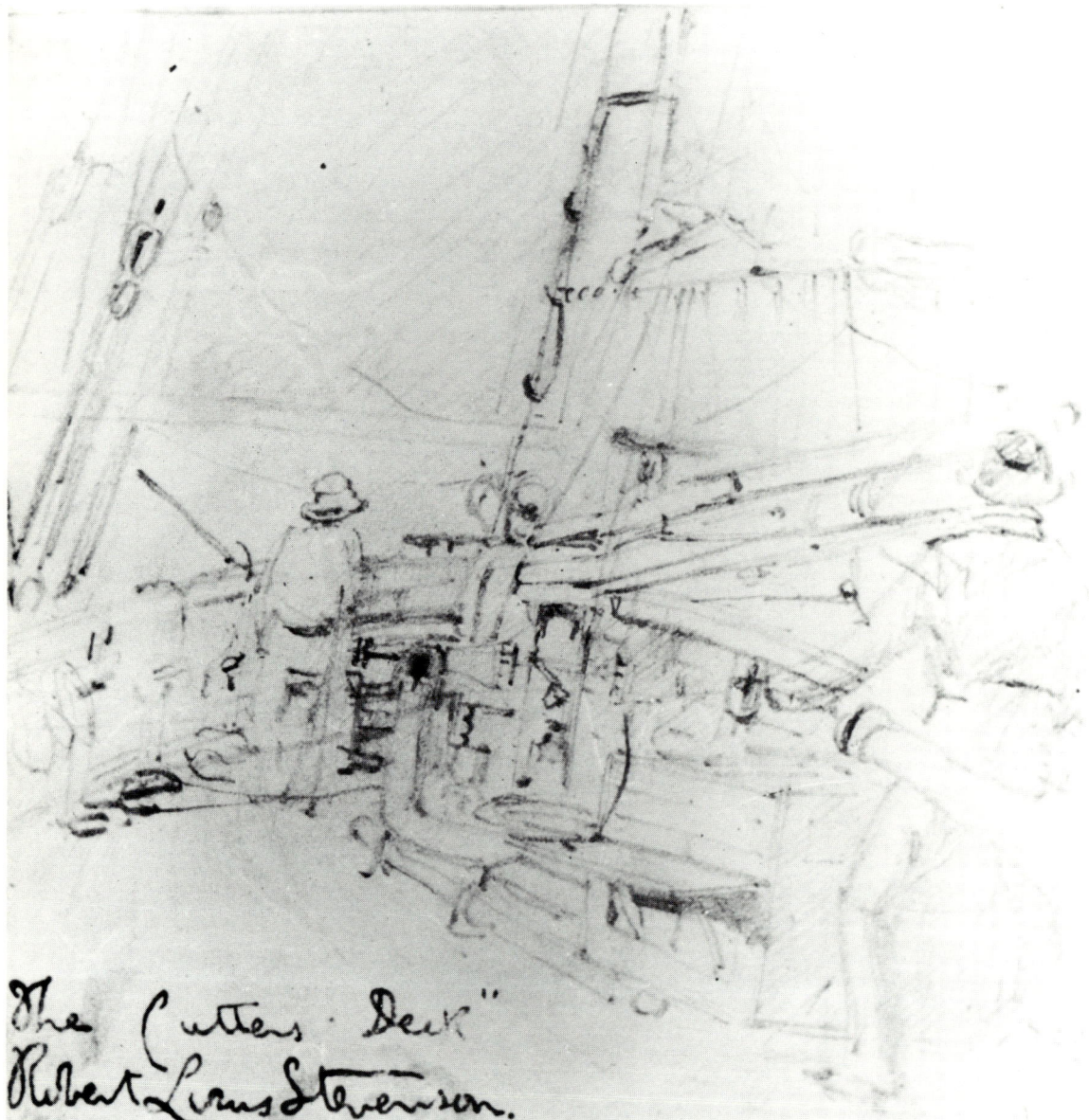

Sketch by R. L. Stevenson

without stockings. Louis goes about in shirt and trousers, and with bare feet; he and Lloyd got their faces and arms so tanned at the beginning that they must now be surely sun-proof. He is up the first in the morning, and is generally the last to go to bed. What do you think of that? . . .

I have seen many flying-fish now, and love to watch them. They look so happy flitting about in the water that one longs to join them in their play. As to our occupations, I have finished a pair of socks for Louis. We are reading Gibbon's *Decline and Fall* and are now in the second volume. Most of it I've to read aloud, as reading in the open air was too much for Louis. We cannot stay on deck in the heat of the day, but it is much cooler below; though once or twice I have been glad to take a siesta. Louis has given up his stateroom because it was too airless, and now sleeps in the fourth berth in the main cabin; so we have turned his room into a dressing-room, and its size permits us to start our indiarubber bath and to have a salt-water 'tub' every morning.

The sailors all have coffee at 6 a.m., as well as any of us who wish for it. Breakfast is at eight. I am generally up at seven and sometimes earlier; once I was even out at five to see the sunrise. After breakfast we all go on deck till Valentine has done up the cabin and made it into a drawing-room once more. After that we 'decline and fall' off, or write and work. At twelve is lunch, and at five dinner. After dinner we go on deck for the sunset, which is the great spectacle of the day. We have had some magnificent ones, but they are about as variable in the tropics as elsewhere and do not always 'come off'. Then we play two rubbers at whist —the captain and I are now eight rubbers ahead; and afterwards we put out the lamps and go on deck to let the cabin cool before going to bed. The evenings are generally delicious, the stars bright, and the air heavenly. We saw the new moon first on Thursday, when it was three days old, but looked very large; though, as Valentine said, when I remarked upon its size, 'Perhaps it was born large'. It may be the way in the tropics! On Friday we had our first peep at the Southern Cross, but unfortunately it was just ahead of the vessel, and partly hidden by the sails, so we cannot be said to have seen it properly yet.

Our little vessel sails splendidly. It is wonderful how she picks her way among the heavy seas and ships so few; but we do get a fair sprinkling of spray now and then. Last Sunday Lou got a regular shower-bath in the cockpit; and I had two lesser ones, one through the skylight in the cabin, and another in the cockpit, one day when it was very stormy. Once, also, when I was sitting in the captain's chair, I was sent spinning across the cabin and struck my head upon the sofa. But see the advantage of a hard Scottish head! I was not hurt in the least, though Louis insisted on banishing the chair, lest another time it might be more serious.

Friday, July 20

In port at last! I cannot tell you how thrilling it was to hear Louis's call of 'Land!' at five o'clock this morning. We fairly tumbled into our dressing-gowns, and rushed on deck. . . .

Yacht Casco, *Anaho Bay, Nuka-hiva, July 22*

This, at last, is my *beau-ideal*! The climate is simply perfect, much more delightful than I could have believed possible so near the Equator. The sun is certainly hot, but there is always a delightful breeze, and it is never in the least sultry or airless. I fancy we have arrived at a fortunate time, as the rainy season is just over and everything is looking new-made and beautiful — *how* beautiful it is hard to make you realise. We all feel as if we wanted to 'draw in our chairs' and stay here a considerable time; even the captain, who was inclined to think the whole expedition quixotic, is charmed. We have an awning over the deck which shades us from the sun, and we spend our whole time when not on shore in the cockpit. At last I have open-air life enough to satisfy even me!

Now I must go back to Friday . . . a large canoe with six or seven natives arrived, bringing cocoanuts, oranges, and bananas for sale. We went on deck to see them, and it was a strange and, to us, rather alarming sight. They were in every stage of undress: two most respectable looking old gentlemen wore nothing but small red and yellow loincloths and *very* cutty sarks on top. There was even some who wore less! The display of legs was something we were not accustomed to; but as they were all tattooed in most wonderful patterns, it really looked quite as if they were wearing open-work silk tights. There was a good deal of bargaining about the price of the fruits, and the wag of the party, who did most of the talking, said it was certainly a very fine vessel, but there seemed to be very little money on board!

Louis took them all over the yacht. . . . They followed him in Indian file, making strange sounds of satisfaction and pleasure all the time. Most of them were distinctly good-looking, but there was one with a very strange, unpleasant face, and an immense mouth that at once suggested cannibalism to us all.

When the chief went on shore, Captain Otis and Lloyd went with him . . . almost as soon as they left us, there arrived two other canoes, and we had presently fourteen natives swarming over the deck. We women were a little frightened, but we made signs that we had no money to buy anything and they soon went away, quite satisfied and apparently not at all surprised. We are told that their own women hold a very inferior position, and are permitted to share very few of the privileges enjoyed by the men. Only very lately has the last *tabu* been removed that forbade the women to walk on roads which men had made, or to use a bridge which men had built; they were compelled, if they desired to cross over, to do so only by wading a creek. Even now they are not allowed to ride in a saddle belonging to a native, though they may use a foreigner's; and as there is only one person in the island who possesses a side-saddle, you may imagine it is in constant request. In some of the other islands, moreover, a woman is not allowed to eat meat; the men form themselves into 'clubs' or parties, where all the pork and other meat is consumed. Would you not think they had taken a hint from civilised society? . . .

Yesterday we had a delightful day. Lloyd, Valentine and I went ashore at 11 a.m., taking bathing-suits and luncheon with us. We found a grove of palm trees for a dressing-room and had a delicious bathe, which reminded me that it was twenty-six years since I had ventured on such a pleasure; but here the water is

Anaho Bay, Nuka-hiva

delightfully warm, and we can stay in as long as we like without risk of chill. After bathing, we lunched on sardines, biscuits and beer, and a native brought us some cocoanuts and oranges, which are a green kind, very juicy and delicious. . . . We saw many of the women while we were on shore, and some of them are very pretty. . . . They wore light-coloured *holakuas* with long trains, a very pretty garment, in which they looked most graceful; their feet were bare but tattooed in such beautiful patterns that they had the appearance of wearing open-work silk stockings. They tattoo their legs all over, and Fanny and I feel naked with our plain white legs when we are bathing. . . .

This morning we had a visit from a much more important chief than ours . . . Kooamua is very intelligent and went all round the yacht, looking at things with a really critical appreciation: everything was carefully and thoughtfully examined. He was greatly pleased with the captain's rifle, did not care much for Lloyd's fiddle; but the thing that charmed him most was the typewriter. He went off at last, very happy, with a *Casco* ribbon for his hat, a piece of plug tobacco in his pocket, and his name and that of every member of his family printed by himself with the typewriter. He looked such a mild and benevolent old gentleman that it is difficult to believe he was till quite recently a cannibal. He is now a wealthy and important man with a large European house in which he entertains the governor; and the French do nothing that concerns the native without consulting him.

The typewritten 'family tree' proved to be so popular that the very same evening our own chief sent us a list of his family to be written out in the same way. Kooamua, however, remained the only one to try the machine for himself. What children they are, happy and contented, with no wants that nature cannot supply. I wonder if we are wise or kind to rouse them to all the cares and anxieties of civilised life. My dear husband used always to say that dogs had much happier lives than ours, and these Kanakas seem as free from every conscious care and responsibility as ever a dog could be. Their conduct to each other and to strangers, so far as kindliness and courtesy are concerned, is much more Christ-like than that of many professing Christians; but I am told that although the Roman Catholic missionaries have been teaching them for a number of years, they have produced very little real effect, save that the islanders have ceased to worship idols. Fanny has secured the last that remained in this bay, a very uncouth attempt at a human figure carved in wood, and in rather a decayed state.

In the South Seas: The Marquesas
An Island Landfall

Few men who come to the islands leave them; they grow grey where they alighted; the palm shades and the trade-wind fans them till they die, perhaps cherishing to the last the fancy of a visit home, which is rarely made, more rarely enjoyed, and yet more rarely repeated. No part of the world exerts the same attractive power upon the visitor, and the task before me is to communicate to fireside travellers some sense of its seduction, and to describe the life, at sea and ashore, of many hundred thousand persons, some of our own blood and language, all our contemporaries, and yet as remote in thought and habit as Rob Roy or Barbarossa, the Apostles or the Caesars.

The first experience can never be repeated. The first love, the first sunrise, the first South Sea island, are memories apart and touched a virginity of sense. On the 28th of July 1888, the moon was an hour down by four in the morning. In the east a radiating centre of brightness told of the day; and beneath, on the skyline, the morning bank was already building, black as ink. We have all read of the swiftness of the day's coming and departure in low latitudes; it is a point on which the scientific and sentimental tourist are at one, and has inspired some tasteful poetry. The period certainly varies with the season; but here is one case exactly noted. Although the dawn was thus preparing by four, the sun was not up till six; and it was half-past five before we could distinguish our expected islands from the

The Needles of Ua-pu, Nuka-hiva

clouds on the horizon. Eight degrees south, and the day two hours a-coming. The interval was passed on deck in the silence of expectation, the customary thrill of landfall heightened by the strangeness of the shores that we were then approaching. Slowly they took shape in the attenuating darkness. Ua-huna, piling up to a truncated summit, appeared the first upon the starboard bow; almost abeam arose our destination, Nuka-hiva, whelmed in cloud; and betwixt and to the southward, the first rays of the sun displayed the needles of Ua-pu. These pricked about the line of the horizon; like the pinnacles of some ornate and monstrous church they stood there, in the sparkling brightness of the morning, the fit signboard of a world of wonders.

Not one soul aboard the *Casco* had set foot upon the islands, or knew, except by accident, one word of any of the island tongues; and it was with something perhaps of the same anxious pleasure as thrilled the bosom of discoverers that we drew near these problematic shores. The land heaved up in peaks and rising vales; it fell in cliffs and buttresses; its colour ran through fifty modulations in a scale of pearl and rose and olive; and it was crowned above by opalescent clouds. The suffusion of vague hues deceived the eye; the shadows of clouds were confounded with the articulations of the mountain; and the isle and its unsubstantial canopy rose and shimmered before us like a single mass. There was no beacon, no smoke of towns to be expected, no plying pilot. Somewhere, in that pale phantasmagoria of cliff and cloud, our haven lay concealed; and somewhere to the east of it — the only seamark given — a certain headland, known indifferently as Cape Adam and Eve, or Cape Jack and Jane, and distinguished by two colossal figures, the gross statuary of nature. These we were to find; for these we craned and stared, focussed glasses, and wrangled over charts; and the sun was overhead and the land close ahead before we found them. To a ship approaching, like the *Casco*, from the north, they proved indeed the least conspicuous features of a striking coast; the surf flying high above its base; strange, austere, and feathered mountains rising behind; and Jack and Jane, or Adam and Eve, impending like a pair of warts above the breakers. . . .

Thence we were borne away along shore. On our port beam we might hear the explosions of the surf; a few birds flew fishing under the prow; here was no other sound or mark of life, whether of man or beast, in all that quarter of island. Winged by her own impetus and the dying breeze, the *Casco* skimmed under cliffs, opened out a cove, showed us a beach and some green trees, and flitted by again, bowing to the swell. The trees, from our distance, might have been hazel; the beach might have been in Europe; the mountain forms behind modelled in little from the Alps, and the forests which clustered on their ramparts a growth no more considerable than our Scottish heath. . . .

Under the eastern shore, our schooner, now bereft of any breeze, continued to creep in. From close aboard arose the bleating of young lambs; a bird sang on the hillside; the scent of the land and of a hundred fruits or flowers flowed forth to meet us; and, presently, a house or two appeared, standing high upon the ankles of the hills, and one of these surrounded with what seemed a garden. These conspicuous habitations, that patch of culture, had we but known it, were a mark of the passage of whites; and we might have approached a hundred islands and not found their parallel. It was longer ere we spied the native village, standing (in the universal fashion) close upon a curve of beach, close under a grove of palms; the sea in front growling and whitening on a concave arc of reef. For the cocoa-tree and the island man are both lovers and neighbours of the surf. 'The coral waxes, the palm grows, but man departs' says the sad Tahitian proverb; but they are all three, so long as they endure, co-haunters of the beach. The mark of anchorage was a blow-hole in the rocks, near the south-easterly corner of the bay. Punctually to our use, the blow-hole spouted; the schooner turned upon her heel. . . .

Before yet the anchor plunged a canoe was already paddling from the hamlet. It contained two men; one white, one brown and tattooed across the face with bands of blue, both in immaculate white European clothes; the resident trader, Mr Regler, and the native chief, Taipi-Kikino. 'Captain, is it permitted to come on board?' were the first words we heard among the islands. Canoe followed canoe till the ship swarmed with stalwart six-foot men in every stage of undress; some in a shirt, some in a loincloth, one in a handkerchief imperfectly adjusted; some, and these the more considerable, tattooed from head to foot in awful patterns; some

'The gross statuary of nature': Omoo Valley

barbarous and knived; one, who sticks in my memory as something bestial, squatting on his hams in a canoe, sucking an orange and spitting it out again to alternate sides with ape-like vivacity — all talking, and we could not understand one word; all trying to trade with us who had no thought of trading, or offering us island curios at prices palpably absurd. There was no word of welcome; no show of civility; no hand extended save that of the chief and Mr Regler. As we still continued to refuse the proferred articles, complaint ran high and rude; and one, the jester of the party, railed upon our meanness amid jeering laughter. Amongst other angry pleasantries — 'Here is a mighty fine ship,' said he, 'to have no money on board!' I own I was inspired with sensible repugnance; even with alarm. The ship was manifestly in their power; we had women on board; I knew nothing of my guests beyond the fact that they were cannibals; the Directory [Findlay's Directories of the World] (my only guide) was full of timid cautions; and as for the trader whose presence might else have reassured me, were not whites in the Pacific the usual instigators and accomplices of native outrage? When he reads this confession, our kind friend, Mr Regler, can afford to smile.

Later in the day, as I sat writing up my journal, the cabin was filled from end to end with Marquesans; three brown-skinned generations, squatted cross-legged upon the floor, and regarding me in silence with embarrassing eyes. The eyes of all Polynesians are large, luminous, and melting; they are like the eyes of animals and some Italians. A kind of despair came over me, to sit there helpless under all these staring orbs, and be thus blocked in a corner of my cabin by this speechless crowd; and a kind of rage to think they were beyond the reach of articulate communication, like furred animals, or folk born deaf, or the dwellers of some alien planet. . . .

Visitors to Casco

Methought, in my travels, all human relation was to be excluded; and when I returned home (for in those days I still projected my return) I should have but dipped into a picture-book without a text. Nay, and I even questioned if my travels should be much prolonged; perhaps they were destined to a speedy end; perhaps my subsequent friend, Kauanui, whom I remarked there, sitting silent with the rest, for a man of some authority, might leap from his hams and with an ear-splitting signal, the ship be carried at a rush, and the ship's company butchered for the table.

There could be nothing more natural than these apprehensions, nor anything more groundless. In my experience of the islands, I had never again so menacing a reception; were I to meet with such today, I should be more alarmed and tenfold more surprised. The majority of Polynesians are easy folk to get in touch with, frank, fond of notice, greedy of the least affection, like amiable, fawning dogs; and even with the Marquesans, so recently and so imperfectly redeemed from a blood-boltered barbarism [cannibalism], all were to become our intimates, and one, at least, was to mourn sincerely our departure.

Letter to Sidney Colvin, Yacht Casco, *Anaho Bay,*
Nuka-hiva, Marquesas Islands, July 1888

My dear Colvin, — From this somewhat (ahem) out of the way place, I write to say how d'ye do. It is all a swindle: I chose these isles as having the most beastly population, and they are far better, and far more civilised than we. I know one old chief, Ko-o-amua, a great cannibal in his day, who ate his enemies even as he walked home from killing 'em, and he is a perfect gentleman and exceedingly amiable and simple-minded: no fool, though.

The climate is delightful; and the harbour where we lie one of the loveliest spots imaginable. Yesterday evening we had near a score of natives on board; lovely parties. We have a native god; very rare now. Very rare and equally absurd to view.

This sort of work is not favourable to correspondence: it takes me all the little strength I have to go about and see, and then come home and note, the strangeness around us. I shouldn't wonder if there came trouble here some day, all the same. I could name a nation that is not beloved in certain islands — and it does not know it! Strange: like ourselves, perhaps, in India! Love to all and much to yourself.

R.L.S.

Letter from Margaret Stevenson to Jane Whyte Balfour
July 28

. . . Yesterday a native dance was got up for our benefit. None of the dancing-women appeared, but five men, nicely dressed in shirts and trousers, danced together with great spirit and grace. The music was provided by a drum made out of an old tin box. Many of the steps reminded me of a Highland reel, but were curiously mixed up with calisthenic, and even gymnastic, exercises: the hands in particular were used very gracefully, and they often took off their hats and waved them to and fro. But they also climbed on each other's shoulders, and did other strange things. After dancing for some time, they sang songs to us in a curious, low, weird kind of crooning. Altogether it was a strange sort of afternoon party!

When we came away . . . we were accompanied by some of the women, who had expressed a wish to visit the yacht; the chief's wife and five others. . . . The mirrors were the things that delighted them most; and this little trait of sex greatly delighted Louis, as none of the men had taken any notice of them at all. One of the ladies had her feet and legs tattooed in really the most wonderful patterns; she was quite pleased when we admired them, and gave us a *most liberal* view of them! At the same time, I must in justice add that they were all perfectly well-behaved and lady-like, though some of the books of travel say that their manners are such that it is impossible for a lady even to land on the island. . . .

In the South Seas: The Marquesas:
Making Friends

I was the showman of the *Casco*. She, her fine lines, tall spars, and snowy decks, the crimson fittings of the saloon, and the white, the gilt, and the repeating mirrors of the tiny cabin, brought us a hundred visitors. The men fathomed out her dimensions with their arms, as their fathers fathomed out the ships of Cook; the women declared the cabins more lovely than a church; bouncing Junos were never weary of sitting in the chairs and contemplating in the glass their own bland images; and I have seen one lady strip up her dress and, with cries of wonder and delight, rub herself bare-breeched upon the velvet cushions. Biscuits, jam and syrup was the entertainment; and as in European parlours, the photograph album went the round. This sober gallery, their everyday costumes and physiognomies, had become transformed, in three weeks' sailing, into things wonderful and rich and foreign; alien faces, barbaric dresses, they were now beheld and fingered, in the swerving cabin, with innocent excitement and surprise. Her Majesty was often recognised, and I have seen French subjects kiss her photograph. . . .

'The Maroon'

On the beauties of Anaho books might be written. I remember waking about three to find the air temperate and scented. The long swell brimmed into the bay and seemed to fill it full and then subside. Gently, deeply and silently the *Casco* rolled; only at times a block piped like a bird. Oceanward, the heaven was bright with stars and the sea with their reflections. . . .

And then I turned shoreward, and high squalls were overheard; the mountains

'I was the showman of the Casco'

loomed black, and I could have fancied I had slipped ten thousand miles away and was anchored in a Highland loch; that when the day came it would show pine, and heather, and green fern, and roofs of turf sending up the smoke of peats; and the alien speech that should next greet my ears must be Gaelic, not Kanaka.

And day, when it came, brought other sights and thoughts. I have watched the morning break in many quarters of the world; it has been certainly one of the chief joys of my existence, and the dawn that I saw with most emotion shone upon the bay of Anaho. The mountains abruptly overhang the port with every variety of surface and of inclination, lawn, and cliff, and forest. Not one of these but wore its proper tint of saffron, of sulphur, of the clove, and of the rose. The lustre was like that of satin; on the lighter hues there seemed to float an efflorescence; a solemn bloom appeared on the more dark. The light itself was the ordinary light of morning, colourless and clean; and on this ground of jewels, pencilled out the least detail of drawing. Meanwhile, around the hamlet, under the palms, where the blue shadow lingered, the red coals of cocoa husk and the light trails of smoke betrayed the awakening business of the day; along the beach men and women, lads and lasses, were returning from the bath in bright raiment, red and blue and green, such as we delighted to see in the coloured little pictures of our childhood; and presently the sun had cleared the eastern hill, and the glow of the day was over all.

The glow continued and increased, the business, from the main part, ceased before it had begun. Twice in the day there was a certain stir of shepherding along the seaward hills. At times a canoe went out to fish. At times a woman or two languidly filled a basket in the cotton patch. At times a pipe would sound out of the shadow of a house, ringing the changes on its three notes, with an effect like *Que le jour me dure* repeated endlessly. Or at times, across a corner of the bay, two natives might communicate in the Marquesan manner with conventional whistlings. All else was sleep and silence. The surf broke and shone around the shores; a species of black crane fished in the broken water; the black pigs were continually galloping by on some affair; but the people might never have awaked, or they might all be dead.

My favourite haunt was opposite the hamlet where was a landing in a cove under a lianaed cliff. The beach was lined with palms and a tree called the purao, something between the fig and mulberry in growth, and bearing a flower like a great yellow poppy with a maroon heart. In places rocks encroached upon the sand; the beach would be all submerged; and the surf would bubble warmly as high as to my knees, and play with cocoa-nut husks as our homely ocean plays with wreck and wrack and bottles. As the reflux drew down, marvel of colour and design streamed between my feet; which I would grasp at, miss, or seize: now to find them what they promised, shells to grace a cabinet or be set in gold upon a lady's finger; now to catch only *maya* of coloured sand, pounded fragments and pebbles, that, as soon as they were dry, became as dull and homely as the flints

Marquesas Islands cannibal chief

upon a garden path. I have toiled at this childish pleasure for hours in the strong sun, conscious of my incurable ignorance; but too keenly pleased to be ashamed. . . .

. . . Fanny and I took the letters to the village, and then went to our usual bathing place, to hunt for shells, bathe, and amuse ourselves generally. About 4.30 the boat came to take us off. As we were returning to the *Casco*, we remarked with some surprise that she had changed her position . . . by the time we had got them all into the boat we were getting very uneasy about the yacht. We could see that she was moving out seawards, and worse than that, seemed to be drifting towards the most rocky and dangerous part of the shore. There appeared to be no one on deck and nothing was being done. We were in a great fright, and got up sail and hurried after her as fast we could; and as soon as we were within hearing, one of our men shouted out, 'You're drifting ashore!' We were all quickly bundled on deck and found the captain, with a very white face, giving orders all round. We took the visitors down to the cabin and kept them occupied there — and I am not sure that it was not the most agonising task; we could hear the bustle on deck, and could follow all that was being done. Another anchor was dropped, a sail hoisted, and a rope attached to the yacht, and some of the sailors getting into the boat, hauled her out from the cliff. . . . The chief and his three brothers-in-law and Lloyd were called up to lend a hand at the windlass, to get up the first anchor, which had fouled, and so was the cause of all the trouble. Fortunately the water is deep close to the cliffs at that point and their efforts were in time; no damage resulted and in about two hours we were comfortably settled in a new and better anchorage, in the centre of the bay just opposite the mouth of it.

At first it had seemed a terrible encumbrance to have so many visitors at such a time, but we were soon very thankful for their help, and indeed should have been very badly off without them. We gave them each a glass of wine, some hard biscuits, half a dollar, and a piece of tobacco to carry away with them, and they were more than content. It appeared that the captain was at supper below, the two sailors at supper on deck. Louis also was on deck, and I think this was the strangest thing of all, for he was admiring the view of a peculiar rocky peak among the mountains, and it struck him that he had not seen it since the day that we entered the bay. Yet he never took fright! It was most providential that we happened to come off just at the time, and in time to warn them.

The strange chief was greatly taken up with my gloves, which he called 'British tattooing'. He smelt them, and made me put them off and on more than once. He was especially delighted with the buttons, and took it much to heart that one had come off. He also admired my sateen dress, and thinks 'shaped' dresses much prettier than *holakus*.

Beach at Anaho

Letter from Margaret Stevenson to Alison Cunningham
Anaho Bay, Nuka-hiva, August 2

My dear Cummy, — . . . Fanny and I are dressed like the natives, in two garments, one being a sort of long chemise with a flounce round the edge, and an upper garment something like a child's pinafore, made with a yoke, but fastening in front [*mumus* and *holakus*]. As we have to wade to and from the boat in landing and coming back, we discard stockings, and on the sands we usually go barefoot entirely. Louis wears only a shirt and trousers with the legs and arms rolled up as far as they will go, and he is always bare-footed. You will not therefore be surprised to hear that we are all as red as lobsters. It is a strange, irresponsible, half-savage life, and I sometimes wonder if we shall ever be able to return to civilised habits again. . . .

Louis is looking so well and has even got a little fatter since we have been staying in this lovely, quiet spot. He sends you his love and bids me tell you that he is just living over all the books you used to read to him. For instance, this morning, when the juice of a cocoa-nut effervesced like ginger-beer, he called out delightedly, 'Oh, I remember Cummy telling me of that long ago, and I thought it so wonderful. And only fancy that poor little sick chap she nursed ever seeing it actually and truly for himself!'

In the South Seas: The Marquesas
Death

. . . When a native habitation is deserted, the superstructure — pandanus thatch, wattle, unstable tropical timber — speedily rots, and is speedily scattered by the wind. Only the stones of the terrace endure; nor can any ruin, cairn, or standing stone, or vitrified fort present a more stern appearance of antiquity. . . . Such ruins are tapu in the strictest sense; no native must approach them; they have become outposts of the kingdom of the grave. It might appear a natural and pious custom in the hundreds who are left, the rearguard of perished thousands, that their feet should leave untrod these hearthstones of their fathers. I believe, in fact, the custom rests on different and more grim conceptions. But the house, the grave, and even the body of the dead, have been always particularly honoured by Marquesans. Until recently the corpse was sometimes kept in the family and daily oiled and sunned, until, by gradual and revolting stage, it dried into a kind of mummy. . . .

Hatiheu

. . . It was what is called a good passage, and a feather in the *Casco*'s cap; but among the most miserable forty hours that any one of us has ever passed. We were swung and tossed together all the time like shot in a stage thunderbox. The mate was thrown down and his head cut open; the captain was sick on deck; the cook sick in the galley. Of all our party only two sat down to dinner. I was one. I own that I felt wretchedly; and I can only say of the other, who professed to feel quite well, that she fled at an early moment from the table. . . .

The port of entry

The port — the mart, the civil and religious capital of these rude islands — is called Tai-o-hae, and lies strung along the beach of a precipitous green bay in Nuka-hiva.

It was midwinter when we came thither, and the weather was sultry, boisterous, and inconstant. Now the wind blew squally from the land down the gaps of splintered precipice; now, between the sentinel islets of the entry, it came in gusts from seaward. Heavy and dark clouds impended on the summits; the rain roared and ceased; the scuppers of the mountain gushed; and the next day we would see the sides of the amphitheatre bearded with white falls. Along the beach the town shows a thin file of houses, mostly white and all ensconced in the foliage of an avenue of green puraos; a pier gives access from the sea across the belt of breakers; to the eastward there stands, on a projecting bushy hill, the old fort which is now the calaboose, or prison; eastward still, alone in a garden, the Residency flies the colours of France. Just off Calaboose Hill, the tiny Government schooner rides almost permanently at anchor, marks eight bells in the morning (there or thereabouts) with the unfurling of her flag, and salutes the setting sun with the report of a musket.

Long-Pig — A cannibal high place

Nothing more strongly arouses our disgust than cannibalism, nothing so surely unmortars a society; nothing, we might plausibly argue, will so harden and degrade the minds of those that practise it. And yet we ourselves make much the same appearance in the eyes of the Buddhist and the vegetarian. We consume the carcases of creatures of like appetites, passions and organs with ourselves; we feed on babes, though not our own; and the slaughterhouse resounds daily with screams of pain and fear. We distinguish indeed; but the unwillingness of many nations to eat the dog, an animal with whom we live on terms of the next intimacy, shows how precariously the distinction is grounded. The pig is the main element of animal food among the islands. . . . Many islanders live with their pigs as we do with our dogs, both crowd around the hearth with equal freedom.

The Marquesans intertwined man-eating with the whole texture of their lives; 'long-pig' was in a sense their currency and sacrament; it formed the hire of the artist, illustrated public events, and was the occasion and attraction of a feast. Today they are paying the penalty of this bloody commixture. The civil power, in its crusade against man-eating, has had to examine one after another all Marquesan arts and pleasures, has found them one after another tainted with a cannibal element, and one after another has placed them on the proscript list. The art of tattooing stood by itself, the execution exquisite, the designs most beautiful and intricate; nothing more handsomely sets off a handsome man; it may coast some pain in the beginning, but I doubt if it be near so painful in the long run, and I am sure it is far more becoming than the ignoble European practice of tight-lacing among women. And now it has been found needful to forbid the art. Their

Place of Sacrifice, Hiva-Oa

songs and dances were numerous (and the law has had to abolish them by the dozen). They now face empty-handed the tedium of their uneventful days; and who shall pity them? The least rigorous will say that they were justly served.

Death alone could not satisfy Marquesan vengeance, the flesh must be eaten . . . they did not dare to hold a public festival. The body was accordingly divided; and every man retired to his own house to consummate the rite in secret, carrying his proportion of the dreadful meat in a Swedish match-box. The barbarous substance of the drama and the European properties employed offer a seizing contrast to the imagination.

House of Temoana

. . Vaekehu lives at the other end of the town from the Residency, beyond the buildings of the mission. Her house is on the European plan; a table in the midst of the chief room; photographs and religious pictures on the wall. . . . Here in the strong through-draught, Her Majesty received us in a simple gown of print, and with no mark of royalty but the exquisite finish of her tattooed mittens, the elaboration of her manners, and the gentle falsetto in which all the highly refined among Marquesan ladies (and Vaekehu above all others) delight to sing their language. An adopted daughter interpreted . . . Vaekehu is very deaf, 'merci' is her only word of French; upon that first occasion, we were conscious of a sense of district-visiting on our part, and reduced evangelical gentility on the part of our hostess. The other impression followed after she was more at ease, and came with Stanislao and his little girl to dine on board the *Casco*. She had dressed for the occasion; wore white, which very well became her strong brown face; and sat among us, eating or smoking her cigarette, quite cut off from all society, or only now and then included through the intermediary of her son. It was a position that might have been ridiculous, and she made it ornamental; making believe to hear and be entertained; her face, whenever she met our eyes, lighting with the smile of good society; her contributions to the talk, when she made any, and that was seldom, always complimentary and pleasing. No attention was paid to the child, for instance, but what she remarked and thanked us for. Her parting with each, when she came to leave, was gracious and pretty, as had been every step of her behaviour. When Mrs Stevenson held out her hand to say goodbye, Vaekehu took it, and then, as upon a kindly afterthought, and with a sort of warmth of condescension, held out both hands and kissed my wife on both cheeks. Given the same relation of years and rank, the thing would have been so done on the boards of the Comédie Francaise. . . . The next moment she had taken Stanislao's arm, and they moved off along the pier in the moonlight, leaving me bewildered.

This was a queen of cannibals; she was tattooed from hand to foot, and perhaps the greatest masterpiece of that art now extant, so that a while ago, before she was grown prim, her leg was one of the sights of Tai-o-hae; she had been passed from chief to chief; she had been fought for and taken in war; perhaps, being so great a lady, she had sat on the high place, and throned it there, alone of her sex, while the drums were going twenty strong and the priests carried up the bloodstained baskets of long-pig. And now behold her, out of that past of violence and sickening feasts, step forth, in her age, a quiet, smooth, elaborate old lady, such as you might find at home (mittened also, but not often so well-mannered) in a score of country houses. Only Vaekehu's mittens were of dye, not of silk; and they had been paid for, not in money, but the cooked flesh of men. It came to my mind with a clap, what she could think of it herself, and whether at heart, perhaps, she might not regret and aspire after the barbarous and stirring past. But when I asked Stanislao — 'Ah,' said he, 'she is content; she is religious, she passes all her days with the sisters.'

Letter from Margaret Stevenson to Jane Whyte Balfour
Yacht Casco *Tai-o-hae, Nuka-hiva, August 17*

. . . Louis, Fanny and I went ashore to call on Queen Vaekehu. She is a most dignified old lady, with quantities of beautiful grey hair brushed back from her forehead. Being slightly deaf, we found it difficult to hold much conversation with her. I am told she was the first person converted to Christianity by Bishop Dordillon. She lives in a pretty wooden house of three rooms a little above the bay, and received us seated in the centre of the middle room. The wooden floors were all spotlessly clean, the walls painted a very pretty turquoise blue. For furniture there were two tables with handsome covers, many chairs, and a few very bad pictures. Through the open door in front had a lovely view of the bay, and the one to the back looked out upon the mountains. . . . An adopted daughter sat beside Vaekehu and acted as interpreter, and brought us also seven coconuts to drink. . . .

On Wednesday, as it was a *fête*-day, there was an early service. . . . The church is quite small, whitewashed inside, and has the usual display of gilding, paper flowers and wax candles. There were nearly a hundred of the girls (from the school), all nicely dressed in white *holakus* and broad-brimmed straw hats trimmed with black ribbon. They looked very neat and were very well-behaved, acting as the choir and singing the service in the crooning, humming native fashion. I can compare the sound to nothing but a gigantic lime-tree full of bees, and I found it so soporific that I very nearly went to sleep . . . a long sermon in Kanaka, in which, by the way, nearly all the service was conducted; and at the close of the Mass about a dozen people took Communion, the queen among them. We were seated beside her majesty and I spoke to her when the service was at an end. She wore a very pretty white *holaku* with three embroidered flounces, a 'cardinal's cape' of black grenadine trimmed with lace, and a leghorn hat trimmed with black ribbon. . . .

In the afternoon (Thursday) Louis, Fanny and I called on Stanislas, [Stanislao] who is the son of the late king and step- and adopted son of Queen Vaekehu. He lives in a wooden house, smaller than her majesty's and it is by no means so nicely kept, neither so spotlessly clean nor so orderly. He is about forty years old, and handsome, in spite of being heavily pockmarked, having had smallpox when it decimated the islands some twenty years ago. His father was one of the many who were carried off by it. Stanislas has been well educated and speaks excellent French, and is evidently both intelligent and sensible. His wife is pretty, but hopelessly untidy. I fancy that our visit had been expected, for no sooner had we arrived than presents were brought out: a piece of *tapa* [native cloth made from tree-bark] for each of us and an old man's beard for Louis. These beards are very highly thought of here, and are difficult to obtain. They are worn by men as ornaments and are fastened on the forehead by a wreath made of porpoise teeth. We were given also green coconuts to drink, which we always enjoy.

Today (Friday) was another busy day. . . . At five we expected Stanislas with

Queen Vaekehu and her adopted daughter

his wife and little grand-daughter, but as his wife was ill and could not come, he brought Queen Vaekehu in her place. This was a great compliment to us, for she had previously told us that she could not manage it, as the rheumatism in her knees made it difficult for her to climb into the yacht; and indeed we could see it was painful for her. She is a delightful old lady, with gentle, caressing manners, very dignified and serene. She wore a thinner white *holaku* than she had worn at church, a white china crepe shawl, and a leghorn hat. She was very kind and courteous to us all, and we liked her very much. . . . They all conducted themselves perfectly at table, and Stanislas talked in a most interesting way and showed us a charming old-time French gallantry —declaring, for instance, that I did not look more than forty! The queen's hands are covered with the finest tattooing I have yet seen, all over the back, like exquisite lace mittens; but I noticed that only the first finger was done, the others being untouched. I asked her son the reason of this, and he shrugged his shoulders and said, 'It is too painful'. When we went on deck, Stanislas said, 'The Kanaka ladies smoke.' Louis went to get a pipe for her majesty, but it occurred to Fanny she might like a cigarette in the Mexican fashion, so she showed her how to roll one. The queen seemed to be delighted with the idea, and copied every movement most deftly. Fanny took a cigarette also to keep her company, and we all sat and smiled and patted each other, in the absence of any mutual language. Meanwhile, Stanislas was going the round of the yacht with Louis and was greatly pleased and interested in everything. I forgot to say the queen brought us presents, a piece of *tapa* for each of us, a finely carved cocoa-nut cup, and another 'old man's beard'.

Monday, August 20

. . . Stanislas invited us to go an excursion today up one of the valleys to see a rocking-stone. He was to provide horses and refreshments; but you may imagine how terribly disappointed we were when the morning turned out hopelessly wet. Saturday also was a rather bad day, the worst since our arrival; but this promised to be much worse. . . .

We intended to leave Tai-o-hae tomorrow, but we may be detained a day or two longer, for our Japanese cook went ashore without leave on Saturday evening, got drunk, and stayed away all night. Yesterday morning, it appears, he was taken up and put in the calaboose till this morning, when he was brought on board and was most insolent to the captain. He may have to be turned off, and it is possible the four sailors may elect to go with him; but we find that we can get others without difficulty and at lower wages. We have already engaged a mate for we found we were 'short-handed' in a storm. . . . If the new sailors are Kanakas, Lou will be delighted as he will be able to get so much information out of them.

'Her leg was one of the sights of Tai-o-hae'

From a letter written on Casco, *August 25*

... After closing your letter on Tuesday, I went ashore to pay farewell visits alone, as Fanny had a headache and could not accompany me. ... In the evening Louis and Fanny went ashore to present their photographs to the queen and Stanislas, and to say goodbye. At parting Louis kissed the queen's hand, which evidently delighted her. ...

In the South Seas: The Marquesas
Two Chiefs of Atuona

... The photographer became aware of a sensation in the crowd and, looking around, beheld a very noble figure of a man appear upon the margin of a thicket and stroll nonchalantly near. The nonchalance was visibly affected; it was plain he came there to arouse attention and his success was instant. He was introduced; he was civil, he was obliging; he was always ineffably superior and certain of himself; a well-graced actor. It was presently suggested that he should appear in his war costume; he gracefully consented; and returned in that strange, inappropriate, and ill-omened array (which very well became his handsome person) to strut in a circle of admirers and be thenceforth the centre of photography. Thus had Moipu effected his introduction, as by accident, to the white strangers, made it a favour to display his finery, and reduced his rival Paaaeua to a secondary *rôle* on the theatre of the disputed village. ...

Moipu formally proposed to 'make brothers' with Mata-Galahi — Glass-Eyes — the not very euphorious name under which Mr Lloyd Osbourne passed in the Marquesas. The feat of brotherhood took place on board the *Casco*. ... Moipu, as if to mark every point to the opposition, came with a certain feudal pomp, attended by retainers bearing gifts of all descriptions, from plumes of old men's beards to little, pious Catholic engravings.

I had met the man before this in the village, and detested him on sight; there was something indescribably raffish in his looks and ways that raised my gorge; and when man-eating was referred to, and he laughed a low, cruel laugh, part boastful, part bashful, like one reminded of some dashing peccadillo, my repugnance was mingled with nausea. ... In his appreciation of jams and pickles, in his delight in the reverberating mirrors of the dining cabin, and consequent endless repetition of Moipus and Mata-Galahis, he showed himself engagingly a child. And yet I am not sure; and what seemed childishness may have been rather courtly art. His manners struck me as beyond the mark; they were refined and caressing to the point of grossness, and when I think of the serene absent-mindedness with which he first strolled in upon our party, and then recall his running on hands and knees along the cabin sofas, pawing the velvet, dipping into the beds, and bleating commendary *'mitais'* with exaggerated emphasis like some enormous over-mannered ape. And I sometimes wonder next, if Moipu were quite alone in this polite duplicity, and ask myself whether the *Casco* were quite so much admired in the Marquesas as our visitors desired us to suppose.

I will complete the sketch of an incurable cannibal grandee with two incongruous traits. His favourite morsel was the human hand, of which he speaks today with an ill-favoured lustfulness. And when he said goodbye to Mrs Stevenson, holding her hand, viewing her with tearful eyes, and chanting his farewell improvisation in the falsetto of Marquesan high society, he wrote upon her mind a sentimental impression which I try in vain to share.

Letter from Margaret Stevenson to Jane Whyte Balfour
Yacht Casco, *Taahaku, Hiva-oa, August 25*

. . . We sailed at 8 a.m. on Wednesday morning and reached our anchorage here at 3 p.m. on Thursday. We had a headwind, and a very high sea; and, as usual, everyone was more or less sick except myself. The captain was very bad indeed, and so was Louis; and our new cook, Au Fou, being also ill, we had to take what food we could get. We passed the island of U-apu during the night and on Thursday morning we were in sight of this island Hiva-oa, which, I am told, means 'Yonder far'. . . . While we were going through the canal, *Frère* Michel pointed out to us two nice large houses that belonged to a 'chieftess', as they say here who adopted him. . . . Fanny and I then said that above everything else we would like to be adopted by a chief; and he declared that nothing was easier, and that when he landed he would arrange for us to be adopted at once.

These islands are much like the others that we have seen, with high mountains sloping up from the beach curiously serrated in outline, and rising here and there to fine abrupt peaks. There are numbers of wooded valleys, and most of the bays have curious detached rocks guarding the entrance which are called 'sentinels'. . . .

On Friday morning Louis got up with a bad headache and looked so wretched that he said he must rest all day. However, he went ashore with us to see if he felt the better of being on land. Fanny, Lloyd and I intended to go to the village, which is at some little distance, to hunt for eggs. . . . We went first to the Keanes who were most kind and hospitable and lent us a horse for Fanny. . . . Lloyd and I walked beside her to the village of Atuona, two miles away, in the next bay. . . . The whole village, it appeared, was *en fête* and charmed with the honour that we were doing them.

Atuona is beautifully situated at the foot of a high and steep mountain, and has more houses gathered together than we have seen in any native village. . . .

Our house (I mean the one belonging to our new parents) is quite magnificent, with no less than three doors and six glazed windows. It is built on a high *pae-pae*, as they call the large stone platforms that support the houses, with a verandah all round, and the windows and doors, as usual, standing wide open. The house is entirely lined with twisted reeds, and the floor covered with matting, and everything was exquisitely clean and fresh. Our new 'papa' was ready to receive us, dressed in a blue coat and white trousers; his name is *Pa-a-a-e-u-a*, and he is a very good-looking man, but more depressed than is general with natives. His wife is quiet and very pleasant, but not good-looking. They have a little adopted child, who was at once introduced to us; he is the son of an Austrian sailor who escaped from a burning ship some fourteen years ago, and who refused ever to go to sea again. He settled down here and married the chief's sister, and this is his son.

While the feast was being made ready, we went to see the pretty little church, where a kind old *père* showed us everything with great pride, and then we visited the mission and the *soeurs*. After this we returned to our house, where we found the tablecloth spread on the floor. It was made of three large banana-leaves, each about four feet long and one and a half wide. On the thick green leaves were laid two dishes of *ka-ku*, a roast chicken, small green onions, water in beer bottles, salt on a small leaf, baked bread-fruit, and cocoa-nut bowls as finger-glasses. Fanny, Lloyd and I sat on the floor, and covered our feet with a corner of the mat, as we had been taught to do at Anaho. Our new father and mother and 'little brother Joseph' seated themselves near us. The roast pig was on the floor behind, and near by, on a round table, was fruit, beer and cocoa-nuts. An elegantly-dressed native stood behind to wait on us, the old *père* beamed most benignantly on us from his chair, and *Frère* Michel, as master of ceremonies, stood beside him. Windows and doors were blocked by interested natives, eagerly watching all the proceedings; and when we could get a peep between them, we caught sight of gaily-dressed women and girls sitting on the spreading roots of a large bread-fruit tree. And the bright sunshine made everything resplendent.

We were offered spoons, but declined, as we wished to show we could be true Kanakas; and, plunging our two forefingers into the bowl, we ate greedily of the *ka-ku*. I asked *Frère* Michel why he did not join us, but he said, 'No, that would not be *convenable*, as I do not belong to your family.' It was, you see, a sort of ceremonial feast, a rite of adoption . . . all that remained to do was for us to give presents to our new relatives. This perplexed us at first, as we had of course come unprepared; but Lloyd took the *Casco* ribbon off his hat, and I gave it to our new 'papa', and Fanny made our 'mamma' happy with a pen-knife. As long as we live we have now a right to come here and share all things with our new family, so you people at home must make yourselves very agreeable if you want to keep us with you! . . .

Frère Michel told us that he was very sorry we could not understand the language and hear the remarks made by the natives. He said they were so gratified by our keeping to the native customs that our popularity was increasing every minute; and the strange thing was that, although we were the observed of all the observers, we all confessed to not having felt in the least awkward or embarrassed. . . . We came back to the yacht, very full of all we had seen and done. Poor Lou was terribly disappointed, however. He said that if we had sent back the horse for him he would have come to the feast even at the risk of having to suffer for it; but this had never occurred to us, as we thought he was feeling too ill to think of such a thing.

August 27

On Saturday our new relatives came to visit us, and we had great discussions as to what presents we should give them. *Frère* Michel told us that they would like a black coat better than anything else in the world, and Lloyd thought he had one that he could spare; but it turned out, unfortunately, that it had been left behind at San Francisco. The captain good-naturedly came to the rescue, and offered us a grey one, with tails. He rather crowed over us, when he saw our difficulties, and declared he was glad that he had not happened to accompany us, and so had no Kanaka parents. After much discussion, however, we ended by giving the 'mamma' a whole piece of print printed calico (forty yards), and a bottle of perfume; and to 'papa' a very nice clasp-knife with a spring to it that Lloyd had bought in San Francisco, a whole box of cigars, and another bottle of scent. Also to 'little brother Joseph' a silk handkerchief, which had been a present to Lloyd. Fanny afterwards added a photograph of herself, and a fan, for the 'mamma'. They all seemed greatly pleased with their presents. . . .

Yesterday afternoon I climbed to the top of a steep hill higher than Arthur's Seat, and had a magnificent view over many lovely valleys and the sea lying

Government House, Nuka-hiva

beyond. This island is more beautiful than Nuka-hiva; but on account of the greater moisture, the climate is perceptibly more trying. We often have regular Scottish mists about the mountains here, and there is such a heavy dew at night we cannot stay late on deck. . . .

Our house at Farakava, Paumotos Islands, September 12, 1888

Louis found the cabin so close on Sunday night that he thought it would be a good plan to take a house by the week, so that he might sleep on shore; and here we are in a dear little wooden erection of three rooms, with a verandah front and back. It is one of the best houses on the island after the Residency. The sitting-room is quite large and airy, with two doors opening on to the verandahs, two windows to the front, one to the back and one at the far end; the two bedrooms open off the other end, and all are painted white, with the doors and windows panelled in blue. In the sitting-room there are two rocking chairs, four round-backed chairs, and a table, and no less than three sewing-machines! (What a pity you are not here!) There are also two brackets on the wall, three framed pictures, a small mirror and a gun. There are wooden bedsteads in the bedroom, small wardrobes, basin-stands, and so on, and actually a copy of David Wilkie's 'Village School' framed and hanging up in one. We were rather afraid of the wooden beds, so we brought ashore our mattresses from the *Casco*, keep them in the bedrooms through the day and at night bring them out and spread them where we please. Usually Louis and Fanny take the front verandah, Lloyd the back, and Valentine and I retire to different corners of the sitting-room, leaving both doors wide open so that there is plenty of air. The only drawback is mosquitoes, but one can't expect absolute perfection in this world. Our house stands beside the little church, but the priest is away just now and there is only a native catechist left in charge. I would fain go to the service, but twenty minutes to six a.m. (when the bell rings) is rather much of a good thing in the way of early rising for me. As it is, the sun wakes us soon after six, and we make breakfast with the help of a paraffin cooking-stove; we have coffee, soup, bread and butter, and marmalade. For lunch and dinner we return to the *Casco*. . . .

The people here are much darker and smaller and not nearly so handsome as the Marquesans; but it is only fair to add that they seem to be better behaved. For instance, the Seventh Commandment is really understood and respected amongst them, and few among them will drink rum to excess, even when they have the chance. In the Marquesas the men cared for nothing else, and the gendarme had to warn us that we must never give them more than *one* glass, however much they might beg for it. . . .

Church at Farakava

Thursday, September 13

Louis was not feeling very well yesterday and wished to get a thorough rest, so Lloyd and I returned on board the yacht and left him and Fanny alone in peace and quiet. . . .

September 16

. . . One disadvantage of a yacht is that everything must be kept so spick and span about her that whenever we are at anchor we live in a chronic state of house-cleaning. All the time we were at Anaho it was going on, and here again we are being repainted, and today two natives have been sitting on a rope in the water cleaning the copper. Then the deck must be holystoned again, and after that has been done we have to wipe our boots with our pocket-handkerchief before we venture on board! We sometimes threaten to go our next trip in a trading schooner or a canal barge in order to escape such trying tidiness. I don't mean to state that we are actually ordered to wipe our boots, but one cannot help entering into the spirit of the thing!

61

Monday, September 17

Yesterday we attended service in the native church and were very much interested. It was 9 a.m. — there were eight men and seventeen women present, including two babies who never made a sound. The catechist was dressed in a black gown with a small cape trimmed with lace; he looked very ministerial, I thought. The service was entirely in the native language, and the people joined in most of it with great interest; a woman acted as clerk and led the singing, which was not bad, but had a considerable nasal twang which reminded me of Gaelic congregations in Arran many years ago. . . .

Tuesday morning

A schooner has just come into the bay, and will take three letters, so I shall finish this and send it off.

Louis was better yesterday, and would have come on board again, but Valentine has a bad cold, and he is afraid of infection; so Lloyd will stay on shore as man-of-all-work to look after the household. Louis is trying to hire a small cutter which belongs to a trader here, to go and see two of the neighbouring islands that have not good enough anchorage for the *Casco*; unfortunately Captain Smith, the owner, is ill, and can't go himself, and he has not yet made up his mind as to whether he can trust his cutter to another person. If we do not arrange this, we shall start very soon for Tahiti, where God grant I may get good news of you all. I do so long for letters after these three months of silence!

Letter to Sidney Colvin
Farakava, Low Archipelago, September 21st, 1888

My dear Colvin, — Only a word. Get out your big atlas, and imagine a straight line from San Francisco to Anaho, the NE corner of Nuka-hiva, one of the Marquesas Islands; imagine three weeks there; imagine a day's sail on August 12th round the eastern end of the island to Tai-o-hae, the capital; imagine us there till August 22nd; imagine us skirt the east side of Ua-pu — perhaps Rona-poa on your atlas — and through the Bondelais Straits to Taakauku in Hiva-oa, where we arrive on the 23rd; imagine us there until September 4th, when we sailed for Farakava, which we reached on the 9th, after a very difficult and dangerous passage among these isles. Tuesday, we shall leave for Taiti, where I shall knock off and do some necessary work ashore. It looks pretty bald in the atlas; not in fact; nor I trust in the 130-odd pages of diary which I have just been looking up for these dates: the interest, indeed, has been *incredible*: I did not dream there were such places or such races. My health has stood me splendidly; I am in for hours wading over the knees for shells; I have been five hours on horseback; I have been up pretty near all night waiting to see where the *Casco* would go ashore, and with my diary all ready — simply the most entertaining night of my life. Withal I still have colds; I have one now, and feel pretty sick too; but not as at home: instead of being in bed, for instance, I am at this moment sitting snuffling and writing in an undershirt and trousers; and as for colour, hands, arms, feet, legs, and face, I am browner than the berry: only my trunk and the aristocratic spot on which I sit retain the vile whiteness of the north.

Please give my news and kind love to Henley, Henry James, and any whom you see of wellwishers. Accept from me the very best of my affection: and believe me ever yours.

THE OLD MAN VIRULENT

Island belles

Market Place, Papeete

Papeete, Taiti, October 7, 1888

Never having found a chance to send this off, I may add more of my news. My cold took a very bad turn, and I am pretty much out of sorts at this particular, living in a little bare one-twentieth-furnished house, surrounded by mangoes, etc. All the rest are well, and I mean to be soon. But these Taiti colds are very severe and, to children, often fatal; so they were not the thing for me. Yesterday the brigantine came in from San Francisco, so we can get our letters off soon. There are in Papeete at this moment, in a little wooden house with grated verandahs, two people who love you very much, and one of them is

ROBERT LOUIS STEVENSON

Letter from Margaret Stevenson to Jane Whyte Balfour
September 26. At sea, on our way to Tahiti.

On Monday we said goodbye to all our good friends at Farakava, and gave them a few farewell gifts. When the captain and I went ashore, we found Taniera [the catechist] sitting with Louis in his working clothes — he is a boat-builder by trade — which consist of blue cotton trousers, and an apron with a bib, leaving an ample stretch of brown satin skin exposed to view. What wonderful skins they all have, by the way! Lloyd introduced him to the captain, saying, 'This is the clergyman of the district; you must shake hands with him'; and I must say the designation and the attire *did* make a very ludicrous combination. When we took leave of Taniera, Lloyd wanted to give him a good present, and the only thing left that we could reasonably do without was a little carriage-clock that I had bought in New York; it had a leather case, and kept excellent time, and was really a wonder for its price. It had originally been intended for giving away; but as all our watches have learnt Kanaka habits and have refused to work in the tropics, we have found the little clock too useful for us to be parted with. However, after an internal struggle which I own was severe, my respect for the church carried the day, and Taniera became its happy possessor.

Government House, Papeete

Tahiti, September 30, 1888

This morning I set off for church, hoping for an English service; but alas! the minister was ill and the church was closed, which was a great disappointment. It appears that there has been an epidemic of influenza here lately; it was brought from Chile, and was of a very severe type; and we are inclined to believe that Louis was somehow infected with it at Farakava. His cough was so bad yesterday that we sent for the doctor, who prescribed some medicine for him that certainly gave him a quiet and fairly comfortable night. It is terribly vexing to us all, when we remember how well he was before this, but I trust he will soon throw it off.

I don't much like Tahiti. It seems to me a sort of halfway house between savage life and civilisation, with the drawbacks of both and the advantages of neither. Also a disagreeable feature of the place is the prevalence of land-crabs. The ground is literally riddled with the large holes made by them. . . . Louis's illness, of course, depresses us all, and keeps us from seeing much or having any desire to do so. . . . Lloyd has attended to those duties that could not well be put off. . . . Two of them [officers of the French man-o-war lying in the bay] have since returned the call and were very polite, but they were amazed when I assured them that I enjoyed being at sea, and seemed to think it most unnatural; no Frenchwoman has ever been heard of who could endure it!

Louis and Fanny moved to the small house I spoke of. . . . You would be surprised to see how comfortable they are, under the circumstances. But the cold is still troublesome, and I grieve to say that the last two days there have been slight threatenings of haemorrhage — nothing to be called serious, but still it is always alarming and distressing. Of course we can make no plans until he is better, and when we may reach Honolulu and get the letters that must be there awaiting us, who can tell? . . .

Letter to Charles Baxter
Taiti, as ever was, 6th October 1888

My dear Charles, — . . . You will receive a lot of mostly very bad proofs of photographs; the paper was so bad. Please keep them very private, as they are for the book. We send them, having learned so [to] dread a fear of the sea, that we wish to put our eggs in different baskets. We have been thrice within an ace of being ashore: we were lost(!) for about twelve hours in the Low Archipelago, but by God's blessing had quiet weather all the time; and once, in a squall, we cam' so near gaun heels ower hurdies, that I really dinna ken why we didnae a'thegither. Hence, as I say, a great desire to put our eggs in different baskets, particularly on the Pacific (haw-haw-haw) Pacific Ocean.

You can have no idea what a mean time we have had, owing to incidental beastliness, nor what a glorious, owing to the intrinsic interest of these isles. I hope the book will be a good one; nor do I really very much doubt that — the stuff is so curious; what I wonder is, if the public will rise to it. A copy of my journal, or as much of it as is made, shall go to you also; it is, of course, quite imperfect, much being needed to be added and corrected; but O, for the eggs in the different baskets.

All the rest are well enough, and all have enjoyed the cruise so far, in spite of its drawbacks. We have had an awfae time in some ways, Mr Baxter; and if I wasnae sic a verra patient man (when I ken that I *have* to be) there wad hae been a braw row, and ance if I hadnae happened to be on deck about three in the marnin', I *think* there would have been *murder* done. The American Mairchant Marine is a kent service; ye'll have heard its praise, I'm thinkin': and if ye never did, ye can get *Twa Years Before the Mast*, by Dana, whaur forbye a great deal o' pleisure, ye'll get a' the needcessary information. Love to your father and all the family. — Ever your affectionate friend.

ROBERT LOUIS STEVENSON

Letter to Sidney Colvin
Taiti, October 16, 1888

. . . We leave here soon, bound for Uahiva, Raiatea, Bora-bora, and the Sandwiches.

> O, how my spirit languishes
> To step ashore on the Sanguishes;
> For there my letters wait,
> There shall I know my fate.
> O, how my spirit languidges
> To step ashore on the Sanguidges.

18th — I think we shall leave here if all is well on Monday. I am quite recovered, astonishingly recovered. It must be owned these climates and this voyage have given me more strength than I could have thought possible. And yet the sea is a terrible place, stupefying to the mind and poisonous to the temper, the sea, the motion, the lack of space, the cruel publicity, the villainous tinned foods, the sailors, the captain, the passengers — but you are amply repaid when you sight an island, and drop anchor in a new world. Much trouble has attended this trip, but I must confess more pleasure. Nor should I ever complain, as in the last few weeks, with the curing of my illness indeed, as if that were the bursting of an abscess, the cloud has risen from my spirits and to some degree from my temper. Do you know what they called the *Casco* at Farakava? *The Silver Ship.* Is that not pretty? . . . I think of calling the book by that name: *The Cruise of the Silver Ship* — so there will be one poetic page at least — the title. At the Sandwiches we shall say farewell to the S.S. with mingled feelings. She is a lovely creature: the most beautiful thing at this moment in Taiti.

Well, I will take another sheet, though I know I have nothing to say. You would think I was bursting; but the voyage is all stored up for the book, which is to pay for it, we fondly hope; and the troubles of the time are not worth telling; and our news is little.

Here I conclude (Oct. 24th, I think), for we are now stored, and the Blue Peter metaphorically flies.

R.L.S.

Letter from Margaret Stevenson to Jane Whyte Balfour
Yacht Casco, Papeete Bay, Tahiti, October 13, 1888

. . . The island is very beautiful, with strangely shaped mountains that remind me of the Giant's Causeway, but still none of us would allow that it came up to the Marquesas; we are faithful still, and I think I always shall be, to our first love in the South Seas. The little steamer that carried us there and back was filthily dirty, and we were all glad to get 'home' to our own clean, bright *Casco* once more, and told the captain we should never again grumble at any amount of wet paint and varnish!

October 19

I am glad to tell you that Louis keeps much better. He has been to lunch at the hotel several times, and for dinner twice although he and Fanny usually have their meals sent in to them. He has also called on the governor, and yesterday he even took a short drive. We had thought of taking a drive right round the island; this, however, we gave up for we did not like to be away four days from Louis, and it would have been out of the question for him. So we decided on some short drives instead, but there is not much variety, as there are only two driving roads.

October 20

. . . We first went to see the tamarind tree planted by Captain Cook; it has been dead for a long time and has been taken possession of by the proprietors of a sort of public-house nearby called '*a l'arbre de Cook*'. We carried off a little piece of the tree, which is fast going to decay, and which is quite unprotected and exposed....

Tautira, Tahiti. November 5, 1888

We left Taravao on Friday morning; and after a rough and rather unpleasant voyage round the peninsula, where everyone on board was more or less ill but myself, we cast anchor inside the reef here at 8 a.m. on Saturday . . . Lloyd brought us tolerable accounts of Louis. He is delighted with his surroundings here, and that is a great matter. He is in the very midst of the large village, and the life of it goes on all around him; the little girls even play special games of hopscotch — or should I call it hop-Tahiti? — before his window to amuse him. The chief, who lives just opposite, has been most kind, and Princess Moe has been really devoted

Native craft, Tahiti

in her attentions. She sometimes cooks dishes herself specially for his dinner, and the chief carries them across with an apron on! One night, when Louis was not at all well, she could not sleep, she was so much distressed about him, and in the morning she insisted upon his moving into her own house, which she has put at his service for as long as he likes. . . . The princess is a delightful creature, and speaks English very well indeed. . . .

November 6

We had a deluge of rain yesterday, which came through the skylight, stopped my writing, and drove me into a corner for shelter. . . . Louis is fairly well again, and is able to go out for a little walk from time to time; but he is terribly thin and white, and has lost all the fine, healthy-looking sunburn that we were so proud of, which disappoints us very much. Still we are very thankful to see him so far better, and we feel that the simple, cheerful life here has helped him very much. . . . This is a very lovely place. High and beautifully-formed mountains sweep close down to the beach, and they are densely wooded to the very top; from the *Casco*'s deck we

Stevenson playing flageolet

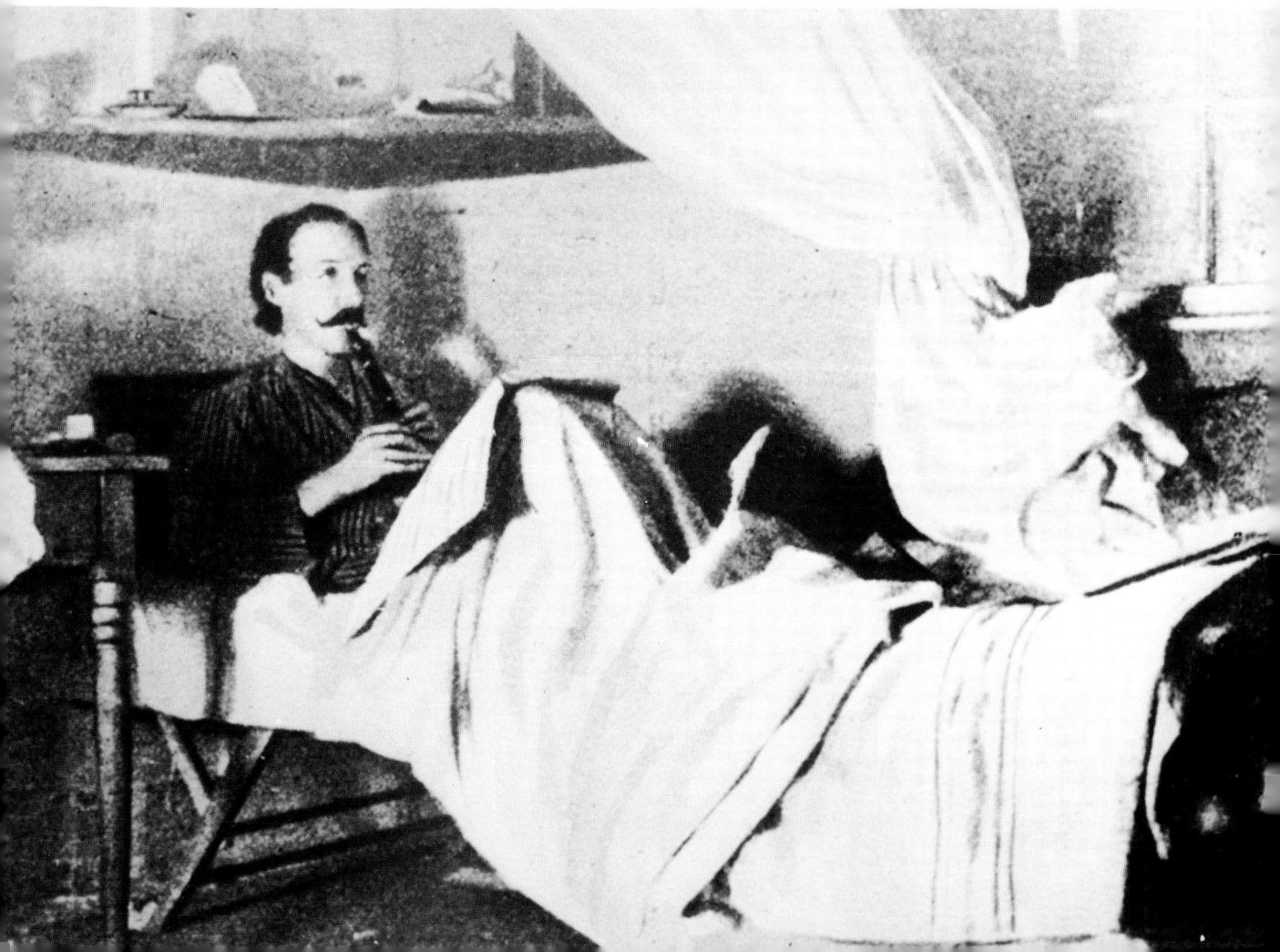

look up a beautiful, winding valley with a cataract tumbling down it, which I long
to visit, but alas! there are no roads save the one to Taravao. We are quite at the
world's end here, in every way; there is not a shop of even the most primitive
kind, which seems strange in so large and populous a village. The people get what
they need from small schooners that come into the bay to trade, and about once a
week, if he has time, the Chinaman from Taravao drives over with bread and
other things for sale. . . .

Fanny is quite *une femme Tahitienne* in her *holaku* and bare feet. She lies on a
pillow in the chief's smoking-room (which is open all round and has a roof of cocoa-
nut bark), and can even take a whiff of a native cigarette and pass it on to the other
members of the company in the approved way. They pass much of the day there,
the ladies generally engaged in plaiting hats of various kinds; I want to get a lesson
in the work, which is pretty and useful, but I have not managed it yet. . . .

On shore at Tautira, Tahiti, 15th November 1888

I little thought when I sent off my letter to you last week that I should write
another from this place. But just after it started the captain discovered there was
something wrong with the main mast of the *Casco*, and after minute examination it
turned out that there was dry rot in it; that it must have been going on for years,
and that it was an actual miracle it did not give way in the gale we encountered
between Papeete and Taravao. The captain is very indignant that the yacht
should have been allowed to start on such a cruise and blames the last captain,
who assured Dr Merrit that the vessel was in perfect order. We feel very thankful
that it was found out before anything more serious happened; and I declare that it
was in answer to the prayers of my kind old ladies that it was discovered before we
went to sea, and indeed on the evening of the very day of my party. . . . It turned
out that no mast large enough for the yacht was to be found in Papeete, so the old
one is to be patched up. The captain declares that it can be made quite safe by the
help of iron rings and bolts. He expects to have everything ready and in order by
the end of next week, when he will return here to pick us up, and we shall start at
once for Honolulu; but this business will make us at least a fortnight later in
getting our longed-for letters. It is fortunate, however, that we are in a place that
we like so much, and where the people are so kind to us, where, in spite of so
much that is strange about us, we still have learnt to feel at home. . . .

I have now sailed all round Tahiti, and driven round half of it. It is certainly a
very beautiful island; the scenery is so varied, and near Papeete is quite park-like
in character, with large and splendid trees, many of them covered with bloom.
The scarlet-flowered acacia was in full beauty and profusion, and was perhaps the
loveliest of all. . . .

Louis's birthday party was a great success. Two small pigs had been
presented to him, and we had them both roasted in a native oven. This way of
cooking certainly preserves all the flavour of the meat and is delicious . . . with

an excellent sauce made of grated cocoa-nut, lime juice, and sea water, Irish potatoes and roast *fei*; after that canned peaches and cake. We also had two bottles of champagne. . . .

Letter to Charles Baxter
Tautira (The Garden of the World) otherwise called
Hans-Christian-Andersen-ville, November 1888

My dear Charles, — Whether I have a penny left in the wide world, I know not nor shall know, till I get to Honolulu, where I anticipate a devil of an awakening. It will be from a mighty pleasant dream at least: Tautira being mere heaven. But suppose, for the sake of argument, any money to be left in the hands of my painful doer, what is to be done with it? Save us from exile would be the wise man's choice, I suppose; for the exile threatens to be eternal. But yet I am of opinion —in case there should be some dibbs in the hand of the P.D. i.e. painful doer; because if there be none, I shall take to my flageolet on the high-road, and work home the best way I can, having previously made away with my family — I am of opinion that if —— [word deleted] and his are in customary state, and you are thinking of an offering, and there should be still some funds over, you would be a real good P.D. to put some in with yours and tak' the credit o't, like a wee man! I know it's a beastly thing to ask; but it, after all, does no earthly harm, only that much good. And besides, like enough there's nothing in the till, and there is an end. Yet I live here in the full lustre of millions; it is thought I am the richest son of man that has yet been to Tautira: I! — and I am secretly eaten with the fear of lying in pawn, perhaps for the remainder of my days, in San Francisco. As usual, my colds have much hashed my finances.

Do tell Henley I write this just after having dismissed Ori the sub-chief, in whose house I live, Mrs Ori, and Pairai, their adopted child, from an evening hour of music; during which I Publickly (with a k) Blow on the flageolet. These are words of truth. Yesterday I told Ori about W.E.H., counterfeited his playing on the piano and the pipe, and succeeded in sending the six foot four there is of that sub-chief somewhat sadly to his bed; feeling that his was not the genuine article after all. Ori is exactly like a colonel in the Guards. — I am, dear Charles, ever yours affectionately.

R.L.S.

Tautira, 10 November 1888

My dear Charles, — Our mainmast is dry-rotten, and we are all to the devil; I shall lie in a debtor's jail. Never mind, Tautira is first chop. I am so besotted that I shall put on the back of this my attempt at words to Wandering Willie; if you can conceive at all the difficulty, you will also conceive the vanity with which I regard any kind of result; and whatever mine is like, it has some sense, and Burns's has none.

Ori a Ori: 'a Roman Emperor in bronze'

Home no more home to me, whither must I wander?
　　Hunger my driver, I go where I must.
Cold blows the winter wind over hill and heather;
　　Thick drives the rain, and my roof is in the dust.
Loved of wise men was the shade of my roof-tree;
　　The true word of welcome was spoken in the door —
Dear days of old, with the faces in the firelight,
　　Kind folk of old, you come again no more.

Home was home then, my dear, full of kindly faces,
　　Home was home then, my dear, happy for the child.
Fire and the windows bright glittered on the moorland;
　　Song, tuneful song, built a palace in the wild.
Now, when day dawns on the brow of the moorland,
　　Lone stands the house, and the chimney-stone is cold.
Lone let it stand, now the friends are all departed,
　　The kind hearts, the true hearts, that loved the place of old.

R.L.S.

Letter to John Addington Symonds

Dear Symonds, — I send you this (November 11th), the morning of its completion. If I ever write an account of this voyage, may I place this letter at the beginning? It represents — I need not tell you, for you too are an artist — a most genuine feeling, which kept me long awake last night; and though perhaps a little elaborate, I think it a good piece of writing. We are *in heaven here*. Do not forget.

R.L.S.

Please keep this: I have no perfect copy.

Tautira, on the peninsula of Taiti

One November night, in the village of Tautira, we sat at the high table in the hall of assembly, hearing the natives sing. It was dark in the hall, and very warm; though at times the land wind blew a little shrewdly through the chinks, and at times, through the larger openings, we could see the moonlight on the lawn. As the songs arose in the rattling Tahitian chorus, the chief translated here and there a verse. Farther on in the volume you shall read the songs themselves; and I am in hopes that not only you, but all who can find a savour in the ancient poetry of places, will read them with some pleasure. You are to conceive us, therefore, in strange circumstances and very pleasing; in a strange land and climate, the most beautiful on earth; surrounded by a foreign race that all travellers have agreed to be the most engaging; and taking a double interest in two foreign arts.

We came forth again at last, in a cloudy moonlight, on the forest lawn which is the street of Tautira. The Pacific roared outside upon the reef. Here and there one of the scattered palm-built lodges shone out under the shadow of the wood, the lamplight bursting through the crannies of the wall. We went homeward slowly, Ori a Ori carrying behind us the lantern and the chairs, properties with which we had just been enacting our part of the distinguished visitor. It was one of those moments in which minds not altogether churlish recall the names and deplore the absence of congenial friends; and it was your name that first rose upon our lips. 'How Symonds would have enjoyed this evening!' said one, and then another. The word caught in my mind; I went to bed and it was still there. The glittering, frosty solitudes in which your days are cast arose before me: I seemed to see you walking there in the late night, under the pine-trees and the stars; and I received the image with something like remorse.

There is a modern attitude towards Fortune; in this place I will not use a graver name. Staunchly to withstand her buffets and to enjoy with equanimity her favours was the code of the virtuous of old. Our fathers, it should seem, wondered and doubted how they had merited their misfortunes; we, rather how we have deserved our happiness. And we stand often abashed, and sometimes revolted, at those partialities of fate by which we profit most. It was so with me on that November night: I felt our positions should be changed. It was you, dear Symonds, who should have gone upon that voyage and written this account. With your rich stores of knowledge, you could have remarked and understood a thousand things of interest and beauty that escaped my ignorance; and the brilliant colours of your style would have carried into a thousand sick-rooms the sea air and the strong sun of tropic islands. It was otherwise decreed. But suffer me at least to connect you, if only in name and only in the fondness of imagination, with the voyage of the *Silver Ship*.

ROBERT LOUIS STEVENSON

[Stevenson met the English poet and critic at the Swiss consumptive clinic in Davos in 1880. Despite a wife and four daughters, Symonds was homosexual and wrote of 'the beautiful companionship of the Shelley-like man, the eager gifted wife and the boy (Lloyd), for whom they both thought in all their ways and hours'. Stevenson described this friendship as 'an adventure in a thornbush, but his mind is interesting'.]

Letter from Margaret Stevenson to Jane Whyte Balfour
Tautira, November 17

. . . Bathing is very fashionable here; but the people all bathe in the river, not in the sea — I can't make out why. The boys and girls climb into the high trees and throw themselves into the water like ripe fruit dropping; they swim like very fishes, and the brown creatures look very pretty as they tumble about. Men and women, boys and girls, all bathe together, but they are all decently clothed in *pareus*; indeed, the people here are very modest and particular in such matters, and no one is allowed to bathe without a *pareu* even in the most secluded spot. The other day I went off by myself to find a quiet place where I might bathe without spectators, but I had not gone far when six children joined in my train. When I had found a nice place with a grove of pandanus trees for a dressing-room, I told the children to go away; they retreated about a couple of yards and then drew themselves up in a line to watch my every movement. It was rather trying, but I used the trees as a screen as best I could; and when the dip was over, they again assisted at my dressing with the greatest interest, and were especially charmed when I took a buttonhook from my pocket and buttoned my boots with it. At present I have a little crowd of boys round about me watching my writing with great eagerness and interest! . . .

Tautira, Thursday, November 23

The Princess Moe arrived on Tuesday. I wanted to give up my room to her, but Ori would not hear of that, and insisted on turning out of the one room he had hitherto kept for their own use; so she is practically living in our house, and we see a great deal of her and like her very much. She has taught us several new plaits for hat-making, and Fanny and she have 'exchanged names' in the native fashion, which is looked on here as a real bond of relationship. She has given Fanny her mother's name, *Terii-Tauma-Terai*, part of which word means 'heaven', I believe, and part is connected with some land in this neighbourhood, and gives Fanny the right to claim it if she has a mind to. In return Fanny gave Moe her own mother's name, which is Hester. Louis and Ori have also 'made brothers' and exchanged names; the name 'Louis' is Rui in the native pronunciation, so that Ori only alters his name very slightly. He has given Louis his own Christian name of *Teriitera*. In making brothers, they have to eat together, but it is not nearly so formal a ceremony here as at Atuona, when we were adopted by the chief, and the feast was only and solely for us and our new family. The princess has also given Lloyd and me complimentary names, but I am not sure of them yet, and will tell you them later.

Letter from Fanny Stevenson to Sidney Colvin
Tautira, Tahiti, December 4th, 1888

Dear, long neglected, though never forgotten Custodian, I write you from fairyland, where we are living in a fairy story, the guests of a beautiful brown princess. We came to stay a week, five weeks have passed and we are still indefinite as to our time of leaving. It was chance brought us here, for no one in Papeete could tell us a word about this part of the island except that it was very

Woman preparing poi-poi

fine to look at, and inhabited by wild people — 'almost as wild as the people of Anaho!'. That touch about the people of Anaho inclined our hearts this way, so we finally concluded to take a look at the other side of Tahiti. The place of our landing was windy, uninhabited except by mosquitoes, and Louis was ill. The first day Lloyd and the Captain made an exploration, but came back disgusted. They had found a Chinaman, a long way off, who seemed to have some horses but no desire to hire them to strangers, and they had found nothing else whatever. The next morning I took Valentine and went on a prospecting tour of my own. I found the Chinaman, persuaded him to let me have two horses and a wagon, and went back for the rest of my family. When asked where I wished to go, I could only say to the largest native village and the most wild. Ill as Louis was, I brought him the next day, and shall never cease to be thankful for my courage, for he has gained health and strength every day. He takes sea baths and swims, and lives almost entirely in the open air as nearly without clothes as possible, a simple pyjama suit of striped light flannel his only dress. As to shoes and stockings we all have scorned them for months except Mrs Stevenson, who often goes barefoot and never, I believe, wears stockings. Lloyd's costume, in which he looks remarkably well, consists of a striped flannel shirt and a *pareu*. The *pareu* is no more or less than a large figured blue and white cotton window curtain twisted about the waist, and hanging a little below the bare knees. Both Louis and Lloyd wear wreaths of artificial flowers, made of the dried pandanus leaf, on their hats.

Moe has gone to Papeete by the command of the king, whose letter was addressed 'To the great Princess at Tautira, P.V.'. P.V. stands for Pomare 5th. Every evening, before she went, we played Van John lying in a circle on pillows in the middle of the floor with our heads together; and hardly an evening passed but it struck us afresh how very much you would like Moe, and we told her of you again. The house (really here a palace) in which we live, belongs to the sub-chief, Ori, a subject and relation of the Princess. He and his whole family, consisting of his wife, his two little adopted sons, his daughter and her two young babies, turned out to live in a little bird-cage hut of one room. Ori is the very finest specimen of a native we have seen yet; he is several inches over six feet, of perfect though almost gigantic proportions, and looks more like a Roman Emperor in bronze than words can express. One day, when Moe gave a feast, it being the correct thing to do, we all wore wreaths of yellow leaves on our heads; when Ori walked in and sat down at the table, as with one voice we all cried out in admiration. His manners and I might say his habit of thought are English. In some ways he is so like a Colonel of the Guards that we often call him Colonel. It was either the day before or the morning of our public feast, that Louis asked the Princess if she thought Ori would accept his name. She was sure of it, and much pleased at the idea. I wish you could have seen Louis, blushing like a schoolgirl, when Ori came in, and the brotherhood was offered. . . .

Let me tell you of our village feast. The chief, who was our guide in the matter, found four large fat hogs which Louis bought; and four cases of ship's

'God's sweetest works — Polynesians'

biscuits were sent over from the *Casco*, which is lying at Papeete for repairs. Our feast cost in all about eighty dollars. Every Sunday all things of public interest are announced in the Farehau (an enormous public bird cage) and the news of the week read aloud from the Papeete journal, if it happens to turn up. Our feast was given on a Wednesday and was announced by the chief the Sunday before, who referred to Louis as 'the rich one'. Our hogs were killed in the morning, washed in the sea, and roasted whole in a pit with hot stones. When done they were laid on their stomachs in neat open coffins of green basket work, each hog with his case of biscuits beside him. Early in the morning the entire population began bathing, a bath being the preliminary to everything. At about three o'clock — four was the hour set — there was a general movement towards our premises, so that I had to hurry Louis into his clothes, all white, even to his shoes. Lloyd was also in white, but barefoot. I was not prepared, so had to appear in a red and white muslin gown, also barefoot. As Mrs Stevenson had had a feast of her own, conducted on religious principles, she kept a little in the background so that her dress did not matter so much. The chief, who speaks French very well, stood beside Louis to interpret for him. By the time we had taken our respective places on the verandah in front of our door, an immense crowd had assembled. . . . All were dressed in their gayest *pareus*, and many had wreaths of leaves or flowers on their heads. The prettiest sight of all was the children, who came marching two and two abreast, the bamboo poles lying lengthwise across their shoulders.

When all the offerings had been piled in five great heaps upon the ground, Louis made his oration to the accompaniment of the squealing of pigs, the cackling of hens, and the roar of the surf which beats man-high upon the reef. . . . Each speaker finished by coming forward with one of the smaller things in his hand, which he offered personally to Louis, and then shook hands with us all and retired. Among these smaller presents were many fish-hooks for large fishing, laboriously carved from mother-of-pearl shell. One man came with one egg in each hand saying, 'Carry these to Scotland with you, let them hatch into cocks, and their song shall remind you of Tautira'. The schoolmaster, with a leaf-basket of rose apples, made his speech in French. Somehow the whole effect of the scene was like a story out of the Bible, and I am not ashamed that Louis and I both shed tears when we saw the enchanting procession of schoolchildren. The Catholic priest, Father Bruno, a great friend of ours, said that for the next fifty years the time of the feast of the rich one will be talked of: which reminds me of our friend Donat, of Farakava, who was temporary resident at the time we were there. 'I am so glad,' he said, 'that the *Casco* came in just now, otherwise I should be forgotten: but now the people will always say this or that happened so long before — or so long after — the coming of the *Silver Ship*, when Donat represented the government.'

In front of our house is a broad stretch of grass, dotted with cocoanuts, breadfruits, mangoes, and the strange pandanus tree. I wish you could have seen them, their lower branches glowing with the rich colours of the fruits hung upon

Supplies Day

them by Ori and his men, and great heaps lying piled against their roots, on the evening of our feast. . . . But there was a day of reckoning at hand. Time after time we ran down to the beach to look for the *Casco*, until we were in despair. For over a month we had lived in Ori's house, causing him infinite trouble and annoyance, and not even his, at that. Areia (the chief — means the Prince) went to Papeete and came back with a letter to say that more work had to be done upon the *Casco*, and it might be any time before she could get to Tautira. We had used up all our stores, and had only a few dollars of money left in Tautira, and not very much in Papeete. Could we stand the journey to Papeete, we could not live upon the yacht in the midst of the workmen, and we had not money enough left to live at an hotel. We were playing cards on the floor, as usual, when this message came, and you can imagine its effect. I knew perfectly well that Rui would force us to stay on with him, but what depressed me the most of all, was the fact of Louis having made brothers with him just before that took place. Had there been a shadow of doubt on our dear Rui's face, I should have fled from before him. Sitting there on the floor waiting for him was too much for my nerves and I burst into tears, upon which the princess wept bitterly. In the meantime the priest dropped in, so that we had him and Moe, and Areia, as witnesses to our humiliating position. First came Madame Rui, who heard the story, and sat down on the floor in silence, which was very damping for a beginning, and then Ori of Ori, the magnificent,

81

who listened to the tale of the shipwrecked mariners with serious dignity, asking one or two questions and then spoke to this effect. 'You are my brother; all that I have is yours. I know that your food is done, but I can give you plenty of fish and taro. We like you, and wish to have you here. Stay where you are till the *Casco* comes. Be happy — *et ne pleurez pas.*' Louis dropped his head into his hands and wept, and then we all went up to Rui and shook hands with him and accepted his offer. . . . Reduced as we were, we still had a few bottles of champagne left. Champagne being an especial weakness of our gigantic friend, it occurred to someone that this was a proper occasion to open a couple of bottles. Louis, the Princess and I were quite, as the Scotch so well say, 'begrutten', Areia's immense eyes were fairly melting out of his head with emotion, the priest was wiping his eyes and blowing his nose; and then for no apparent cause we suddenly fell to drinking and clinking glasses quite merrily: the bewildered attendant clinked and drank too, and then sat down and waited in case there should be any repetition of the drinking part of the performance. And sure enough there was, for in the midst of an animated discussion as to ways and means, Mrs Stevenson announced that it was St Andrew's Day, so again the attendant clinked and drank with Ori's mad foreigners.

It is quite true that we live almost entirely upon native food, our luncheon today consisted of raw fish with sauce made of cocoanut milk mixed with sea water and lime juice, taro *poi-poi*, and bananas roasted in hot stones in a little pit in the ground with cocoanut cream to eat with them. Still we like coffee in the evening, a little wine at dinner, and a few other products of civilisation. It would be possible, the chief said, to send a boat, but that would cost sixty dollars. A final arrangement, which we were forced to accept, was that Rui should go in his own boat, and the chief would appoint a substitute for some public work that he was then engaged upon. Early the next morning, amidst a raging sea and a storming wind, Rui departed with three men to help him. It is forty miles to Papeete and Rui, starting in the early morning, arrived there at nine o'clock; but alas the wind was against him, and it was altogether six days before he got back. . . .

Louis has done a great deal of work on his new story, *The Master of Ballantrae*, almost finished it, in fact, while Mrs Stevenson and I are deep in the mysteries of hat-making, which is a ladies' accomplishment taking the place of water-colour drawing in England. It is a small compliment to present a hat to an acquaintance. Altogether we have about thirteen. Next door to us is Areia's out-of-door house, where he and the ladies of his family sleep and eat; it has a thatched roof of palm branches, and a floor of boards, the sides and ends being open to the world. On the floor are spread mats plaited of pandanus leaves, and pillows stuffed with silk cotton from the cotton tree. We make little calls upon the ladies, lie upon the mats, and smoke cigarettes made of tobacco leaves rolled in a bit of dried pandanus, and admire their work or get a lesson; or they call upon us and lie upon our mats. One day there was an election in the Farehau. . . . In the beginning, the

French deposed the born chiefs and told the people to elect men for themselves. The choice of Tautira fell upon Rui, who declined the honour, saying that Areia was his natural chief and he could not take a position that should belong to his superior; upon which the people elected Areia chief and Rui sub-chief and head councillor. . . . The Farehau is an immense bird-cage of bamboos tied together with pandanus fibre and thatched with palms. In front of the dais the ground is deeply covered with dried leaves. The costume of the dignitaries was rather odd. Areia wore a white shirt and blue flannel coat, which was well enough; but on his plump legs were a pair of the most incredible trousers; light blue calico with a small red pattern, such as servant girls wear for gowns in England: on his feet were neat little shoes and stockings. Rui was a fine sight, and we were very proud of him; he sat, exactly like an English gentleman, holding himself well in hand, alert as a fox and keen as a greyhound; several men spoke from the farther end of the hall, making objections of some sort, we could see. Rui listened with a half satirical, half kindly smile in his eyes, and then dropped a quiet answer without rising from his seat, which had the effect of raising a shout of laughter and quite demolishing his opponent. Voters came up to the table and dropped their bits of paper into a slit in a box. . . . Both Lloyd and I grew very sleepy and as we did not like to leave till the election was decided, we just threw ourselves down and took a nap at the feet of the councillors: nor did we wake till the chief called out to us in English: 'It is finished.' I never thought I should be able to calmly sleep at a public meeting on a platform in the face of several hundred people: but it is wonderful how quickly one takes up the ways of a people when you live with them as intimately as we do.

I hear dinner coming on the table, so with much love from us all to you and other dear ones, including our dear friend Henry James, believe me, affectionately yours.

FANNY V. de G. STEVENSON

Letter from Margaret Stevenson to Jane Whyte Balfour
Tautira, Tahiti. December 4, 1888

On Sunday afternoon, there was an extra long discussion after church service, when several evidently amusing remarks were made and much applauded. In the evening I asked Moe many questions about it all; it appears that on these occasions all the three sermons they have heard in the day are discussed and criticised, and the minister asks questions to see if they have listened and understood the meaning. It seems to me an excellent plan for keeping their attention and interest, and I should like to see it introduced into some country places at home. I asked also what the jokes had been. She told me that one of the sermons was about Nebuchadnezzar, and apparently his being made to eat grass like the beast, as a punishment for pride, had provoked most of the laughter. Louis here broke in rather flippantly, and asked the princess, 'Where was Moses when the candle went out?' . . . Our deacon put several questions, which we managed to answer with some credit; and then he asked what was the reason of the 'shaved heads' of the Roman Catholic priests, and started Louis on the ancient history of the tonsure. . . .

December 5

The high wind still continues, and there is no saying when Ori may get back. We only hope he is safe at Papeete, where there are said to be six boats from Tautira and six from Taravao, all waiting at Point Venus for a change of wind, and unable to get home till it comes. We are more than vexed that Ori should go through all this on our account; everyone made sure of a change in the weather on Monday, with the new moon; but we were disappointed in our hopes. Meanwhile we are all perforce teetotallers, having nothing left of a spiritous character save a bottle of very new rum that Ori gave us; the taste of which, to the unaccustomed palate, is so very unpleasant that nothing short of the direst necessity will induce us to touch it.

I think what we suffer most from, however, is the want of books. I have only one with me, and Lloyd had none at all, so he has shared mine, and I am sure has read it two or three times entirely through. I said to him one day that I thought he could pass an examination in it now, and he replied, 'Yes, if I just crammed up a few dates and some of the pieces of poetry, I could go in for a first class with honours.' It is the *Life of Sir Henry Lawrence*, and very interesting, but I have no doubt you have read it.

December 8

Ori came back in safety on Thursday evening, bringing our stores, so we are relieved about him and no longer feel like shipwrecked mariners. He was greatly delighted with his visit to the *Casco*; he had lived on board from Saturday till Monday and declared that it was 'just like having a father at Papeete'. . . .

December 16

. . . This has been another Communion Sunday here. . . . I little thought that I should have another opportunity of 'keeping the feast' with my good friends, but so it has been, and much shaking of hands we had when all was over. How often I shall remember it when I am far away!

Fanny has turned this house into a veritable picture-gallery. First she did a silhouette of Ori by taking the shadow of his head on the wall, with the help of a lamp, drawing the outline and then filling it in with Indian ink. This was for us to carry away with us; but it turned out so good that Ori demanded to have all *our* likenesses in return, and she has been hard at work to satisfy him, Lou doing the

'R.L.S.'

outline of her own head for her. All are really good but I think mine is the greatest success of the lot and I wished my dear T. could have seen it. He was never quite satisfied with what he called 'ordinary' photographs of me! Louis has printed under them all our names, both in English and native. On his own he has put 'Teriitera, Robert Louis Stevenson, and party, came ashore from yacht *Casco*, November 1888; and were two months the guests of Ori, to whom, having little else, they gratefully bequeathed their shadows in memoriam'. Under Fanny's various names is added, 'Made these shadows for the house of Ori the tall, December 1888'.

On board the Casco, *at sea, December 27*

... After church a number of the congregation came to say goodbye, sitting round the room and on the verandah, as sad and solemn as if they were at a funeral. We only managed to slip out for a few minutes to snatch a farewell visit to *Père* Bruno and the chief. At 11.30 the captain came with the boat to take us off, our final adieus had to be said, and we tore ourselves sorrowfully away from the kind friends and the lovely place where we had spent two happy months. Heavy rain came on after we got on board; but in spite of that, Ori and many of the people, both young and old, gathered under the trees, at the place whence they could watch our departure. It was about 2.30 before all was ready and the wind favourable; we then weighed anchor, and as we passed out through the reef the captain fired thirteen shots from his rifle and the flag was thrice dipped in a farewell salute. Seven shots were fired from the shore in answer, and we replied with another three: while we all stood on deck frantically waving our handkerchiefs to the friends whom we could still see watching us. We could not tear ourselves away till they were quite out of sight. The rain was over by this time, and the sun shone on our departure; but it was a very sad Christmas Day, and we do not wish to make so long a stay at any other place — it makes the parting too trying. We did our best to cheer up at dinner, and had a game of whist in the evening, but it was half-hearted work.

I must tell you, while I think of it, a *bon mot* of Ori's. Louis was telling him about his father and the 'Northern Lights'; when Ori, with a wave of his hand towards the portraits, immediately said, '*He* made lights, and *she* (Fanny) makes shadows.' . . . One evening he asked Louis how much he made by his books, and when he was told what *Kidnapped* brought in the first year, he could not believe that there was not some mistake, and though it was 10 p.m. went off to bring the chief as interpreter, and make *sure*. As they scarcely read themselves, it must be strange and almost incredible to them that book-making should be a paying occupation! . . .

The other thing is that this same *Père* Bruno is going to take Louis as the text of the sermon! I think this should delight Cummy's heart when she hears of it, and I wonder how often Lou is to appear in the pulpit, either in person, or through his books. This time he is to be held up to the people of Tautira because he was so cheerful and uncomplaining during his stay there, 'though he had to put up with many things that must have been hardships to him'; and then his style of dress is to be held up as an example: 'he only wore what was useful and necessary, and never went in for anything ornamental or extravagant'!! Louis is delighted that he has *at last* found someone who appreciates his taste in dress, and wishes he could have a copy of the sermon to send to some of his scoffing friends. *I* may here

Stevenson with guest

privately mention that I think his dress should rather have been held up as a beacon to warn than an example to imitate, seeing that he seldom wore anything but a pyjama suit intended only for sleeping in, very badly shaped, and *dreadfully* unbecoming!

Well, we spent nine weeks in all at Tautira, and so far as Lou's health is concerned, the long detention has proved a blessing. The change in him is something marvellous; all the first week he was in bed with constant cough, high fever, and all the worst symptoms, and now he is better than I have known him since 1879, is able for a good long walk, and has been for some time bathing in the sea almost every day. His appetite, too, has been splendid — he has been able to write a good deal and has nearly finished *The Master*, and we think and hope that he is a little fatter even than when he was in the Marquesas, which was the highest level he had hitherto reached. All this makes us start our journey northward — and the long-run homeward — in a very thankful frame of mind.

January 1, 1889

Another lovely night after a hot summer day. It is hard to believe that this is New Year's Day, and harder to realise what this day was last year at Saranac, when we shivered amidst the surrounding snows. How like a dream that part of our trip seems now!

We had a very quiet day, and the only notable event was that we had stewed duck for lunch, the last of our fresh meat. Louis dined with us — he generally takes his meals in the after cabin for the sake of greater coolness — and our dinner consisted of salt beef, salt pork, a stew of tinned mutton, vegetables, duff, and champagne, in which you may be sure we drank to you all at home. In the evening, as a mild excitement, we played 'what is my thought like' in the starlight. I am sorry to say, however, that they promise us a change of weather with the new moon.

January 6

That promised change came, with a vengeance. Since Tuesday night the weather has been very unpleasant, squalls of wind, rain pouring as it only can in the tropics, thunder and lightning, hail and gloom. For two whole days we were shut up in the cabin, and got through the time as best we could with the help of Gibbon, hat-plaiting and cards. I am also reading Lawrence's life and enjoying it very much. . . . We ought to be nearing Honolulu (and our letters!) by this time. . . . I wonder how our stores, at any rate of luxuries, will hold out. When we left Tautira, Ori gave us a boatload of fruit and vegetables, which have been a great boon, but unfortunately the rain has spoiled the bananas and the mangoes too are on their last legs. The vegetables are almost finished, but we still have cocoanut cream for our coffee.

Letter to Sidney Colvin
Yacht Casco, *at sea, 14th January 1889*

My dear Colvin, — Twenty days out from Papeete. Yes, sir, all that, and only (for a guess) in 4 degrees north or at the best 4 degrees 30′, though already the wind seems to smell a little of the north Pole. My handwriting you must take as you get, for we are speeding along through a nasty swell, and I can only keep my place at the table by means of a foot against the divan, the unoccupied hand meanwhile gripping the inkbottle. As we begin (so very slowly) to draw near to seven months of correspondence, we are all in some fear; and I want to have letters written before I shall be plunged into that boiling pot of disagreeables which I constantly expect at Honolulu. What is needed can be added there.

We were kept two months at Tautira in the house of my dear old friend, Ori a Ori, till both the masts of this invaluable yacht had been repaired. It was all for the best; Tautira being the most beautiful spot, and its people the most amiable I have ever found. Besides which, the climate suited me to the ground; I actually went sea-bathing almost every day, and in our feasts (we are all huge eaters in Taiarapu) have been known to apply four times for pig. And then again I got wonderful materials for my book, collected songs and legends on the spot; songs still sung in chorus by perhaps a hundred persons, not two of whom can agree on their translation; legends, on which I have seen half a dozen seniors sitting in conclave and debating what came next. Once I went a day's journey to the other side of the island to Tati, the high chief of the Tevas — *my* chief, that is, for I am now a Teva and Teriitera, at your service — to collect more and correct what I had already. In the meanwhile I got on with my work, almost finished *The Master of Ballantrae*, which contains more human work than anything of mine but *Kidnapped*, and wrote the half of another ballad, the *Song of Rahero*, on a Taiarapu legend of my own clan, sir — not so much fire as the *Feast of Famine*, but promising to be more even and correct. But the best fortune of our stay at Tautira was my knowledge of Ori himself, one of the finest creatures extant. The day of our parting was a sad one. We deduced from it a rule for travellers: not to stay two months in one place — which is to cultivate regrets.

At last our contemptible ship was ready; to sea we went, bound for Honolulu and the letter-bag, on Christmas Day; and from then to now have experienced every sort of minor misfortune, squalls, calms, contrary winds and seas, pertinacious rains, declining stores. Here is a page of complaint, when a verse of thanksgiving had perhaps been more in place. For all this time we must have been skirting past dangerous weather, in the tail and circumference of hurricanes, and getting only annoyance where we should have had peril, and ill-humour instead of fear.

I wonder if I have managed to give you any news this time, or whether the usual damn hangs over my letter? 'The midwife whispered, be thou dull!' or at least inexplicit. Anyway I have tried my best, am exhausted with the effort, and fall back into the land of generalities. I cannot tell you how often we have planned our arrival at the Monument:* two nights ago, the 12th January, we had it all planned out, arrived in the lights and whirl of Waterloo, hailed a hansom, span up Waterloo Road, over the bridge, etc. etc. and hailed the Monument gate in triumph and with indescribable delight. My dear Custodian, I always think we are too sparing of assurances: Cordelia is only to be excused by Regan and Goneril in the same nursery; I wish to tell you that the longer I live, the more dear do you become to me; nor does my heart own any stronger sentiment. If the bloody schooner didn't send me flying in every sort of direction at the same time, I would say better what I feel so much; but really, if you were here, you would not be writing letters, I believe; and even I, though of a more marine constitution, am much perturbed by this bobbery and wish — O ye gods, how I wish! — that it was done, and we had arrived, and I had Pandora's Box (my mailbag) in hand, and was in lively hope of something eatable for dinner instead of salt horse, tinned mutton, duff without any plums, and pie fruit which now make up our whole repertory. O Pandora's Box! I wonder what you will contain. As like as not you will contain but little money: if that be so, we shall have to retire to 'Frisco on the *Casco* and thence by sea *via* Panama to Southampton, where we should arrive in April. I would like fine to see you on the tug: ten years older both of us than the last time you came to welcome Fanny and me to England. If we have money, however, we shall do a little differently: send the *Casco* away from Honolulu empty of its high-born lessees, for that voyage to 'Frisco is one long dead beat in foul and at least in cold weather; stay a while behind, follow by steamer, cross the States by train, stay a while in New York on business, and arrive probably by the German Line in Southampton. But all this is a question of money. We shall have to lie very dark a while to recruit our finances: what comes from the book of the cruise, I do not want to touch until the capital is repaid.

R.L.S.

[*Colvin's house near the British Museum.*]

Letter from Margaret Stevenson to Jane Whyte Balfour
January 20

On Thursday we got fairly into the Trades, and have been flying along at a great rate ever since, making 170 miles in the first twenty-four hours, and 230 in the twenty-four ending today. But I cannot call it 'pleasure sailing', as it has been a 'beam sea' all the time, and we are tired out with the constant holding-on and

Diamond Head, Honolulu

effort required to keep oneself fairly steady. Such a knocking-about is very fatiguing after a time, and there is no rest night or day. The spray comes over so much that it is almost impossible to sit in the cockpit; and last night, though only a small bit of the lee side of the cabin skylight was open, a bucket of water poured itself straight on my head at 3.30 this morning, and I awoke, screaming and soaked. I took refuge on the floor, and presently saw the same thing exactly happen to Lloyd. Fanny suffers a good deal from seasickness, and declares that when only she reaches Honolulu she is going *ashore* and never means to leave it again. The captain has bad earache in both ears, so we shall not be sorry when the voyage comes to an end, which we hope it may do by Tuesday. And then for six months' supply of letters and papers! . . . One thing we have all realised lately, and that is the loneliness of this great ocean; we have been four weeks out and have only seen a single sail. It gives one some idea of the hopelessness of expecting help should anything go wrong, and makes one more than ever thankful for our safety hitherto.

Tuesday, January 22

Yesterday morning at 10.30 we sighted Hawaii, a lofty mountain with white clouds wreathed about it, above which its head was lifted. We were spinning along at such a rate that the captain quite thought we should reach Honolulu by the evening, and we were pleasantly excited. But alas, when we got under the lee of the land the wind fell; and this morning we are becalmed and only a little further north than the bay where Captain Cook was murdered. This side of Hawaii is very bleak and treeless, with high cliffs, and it is hard to be stopped when we are so near port, but I am thankful to say our food supplies have held out. That is to say, we have still salt beef and macaroni and tinned tomatoes, and pickles and jam; and we have a *very* little flour and coffee and sugar. But the captain is suffering much from earache, and both Louis and Valentine are threatened with the same, so you may imagine how we long to 'get in'.

Wednesday, 1 p.m. We are slowly drawing nearer to Honolulu. We have now three small islands on our right, Maui, Lanai, and that sad tomb of the living, Molokai; and far ahead we can see the very striking outline of Oahu. We hope to land in time for dinner, and are longing for some fresh food and our letters. God grant this long-awaited news of you all may be good news and happy.

The Stevensons' arrival at Royal Hawaiian Hotel

Royal Hawaiian Hotel

After all it was 3 p.m. on Thursday 24th before the calms allowed us to cast anchor in the harbour of Honolulu. Our luncheon that last day consisted of salt beef and biscuits, for all else had given out; so you see we narrowly escaped 'starvation diet', and I must confess our dinner that night at the hotel seemed to be the very finest banquet of which I had ever partaken. But, oh dear me, this place is so civilised! And to come back from Tautira to telephones and electric light is at first very bewildering and unpleasant. I grant the conveniences, but we realise that our happy cruise in the South Seas has come to an end. Thank God, the end is a happy one, and we are met by good news of all we love. But it is the end, nevertheless.

Letter to E. L. Burlingame
(Editor of Scribner's Magazine, New York)
Honolulu, January 1889

My dear Burlingame, — Here at last I have arrived. We could not get away from Tahiti till Christmas Day and then had thirty days of calms and squalls, a deplorable passage. This has thrown me all out of gear in every way. I plunge into business. . . . Tomorrow the mail comes in, and I hope it will bring me money either from you or home, but I will add a word on that point.

My address will be Honolulu — no longer yacht *Casco*, which I am packing off — till probably April.

Henry the Trader has not yet turned up: I hope he may tomorrow, when we expect a mail. Not one word of business have I received either from the States or England, nor anything in the shape of coin; which leaves me in a fine uncertainty and quite penniless on these islands. H.M. [King Kalakaua] (who is a gentleman of a courtly order and much tinctured with letters) is very polite; I may possibly ask for the position of palace doorkeeper. My voyage has been a singular mixture of good and ill-fortune. As far as regards interest and material, the fortune has been admirable; as far as regards time, money, and impediments of all kinds, from

Joe Strong, Stevenson and King Kalakaua

With King Kalakaua

His Hawaiian Majesty

squalls and calms to rotten masts and sprung spars, simply detestable. I hope you will be interested to hear of two volumes on the wing. The cruise itself, you are to know, will make a big volume with appendices; some of it will first appear as (what they call) letters in some of M'Clure's papers. I believe the book when ready will have a fair measure of serious interest: I have had great fortune in finding old songs and ballads and stories, for instance, and have many singular instances of life in the last few years among these islands. . . . To resume my desultory song, I desire you would carry the same fire (hereinbefore suggested) in your decision on *The Wrong Box*; for in my present state of benighted ignorance as to my affairs for the last seven months — I know not even whether my house or my mother's house have been let — I desire to see something definite in front of me — outside the lot of palace doorkeeper. I believe the said *Wrong Box* is a real lark; in which, of course, I may be grievously deceived; but the typewriter is with me. . . .

R.L.S.

[To King Kalalaua from R.L.S.: presented to the King during the Waikiki laua on February 3, 1889 together with the gift of a mounted gold pearl from the Tuamoto Islands. The Silver Ship is the yacht *Casco*.]

From 'Ballads and Other Poems'

The Silver Ship, my King — that was her name
In the bright islands whence your fathers came —
The Silver Ship, at rest from winds and tides,
Below your palace in your harbour rides:
And the seafarers, sitting safe on shore,
Like eager merchants count their treasures o'er.

One gift they find, one strange and lovely thing,
Now doubly precious since it pleased a king.
The right, my liege, is ancient as the lyre
For bards to give to kings what kings admire.
'Tis mine to offer for Apollo's sake;
And since the gift is fitting, yours to take.
To golden hands the golden pearl I bring:
The ocean jewel to the island king.

Letter to Charles Baxter
Honolulu, February 8th, 1889

My dear Charles, — Here we are at Honolulu, and have dismissed the yacht, and lie here till April anyway, in a fine state of haze, which I am yet in hopes some letter of yours (still on the way) may dissipate. No money, and not one word as to money! However, I have got the yacht paid off in triumph, I think; and though we stay here impignorate, it should not be for long, even if you bring us no extra help from home. The cruise has been a great success, both as to matter, fun and health; and yet, Lord, man! we're pleased to be ashore! Yon was a very fine voyage from Tahiti up here, but — the dry land's a fine place too, and we don't squalls any longer, and eh, man, that's a great thing. Blow, blow, thou wintry wind, thou hast done me no appreciable harm beyond a few grey hairs! Altogether, this foolhardy venture is achieved; and if I have but nine months of life and any kind of health, I shall have both eaten my cake and got it back again with usury. But, man, there have been days when I felt guilty, and thought I was in no position for the head of a house.

Your letter and accounts are doubtless at S.F. and will reach me in course. My wife is no great shakes; she is the one who has suffered most. My mother had had a Huge Old Time; Lloyd is first chop; I so well that I do not know myself — sea-bathing, if you please, and it is far more dangerous, entertaining and being entertained by His Majesty here, who is a very fine intelligent fellow, but O, Charles, what a crop for the drink. He carries it, too, like a mountain with a sparrow on its shoulders. We calculated five bottles of champagne in three hours and a half (afternoon) and the sovereign quite presentable, although perceptibly more dignified at the end. . . .

The extraordinary health I enjoy and variety of interests I find among these islands would tempt me to remain here; only for Lloyd, who is not well placed in such countries for a permanency; and a little for Colvin, to whom I feel I owe a sort of filial duty. And these two considerations will no doubt bring me back — to go to bed again — in England. Yours ever affectionately,

R.L.S.

Letter to his cousin, R. A. M Stevenson
Honolulu, February 1889

My dear Bob, — My extremely foolhardy venture is practically over. How foolhardy it was I don't think I realised. We had a very small schooner and, like most yachts, over-rigged and over-sparred, and like many American yachts on a very dangerous sail plan. The waters we sailed in are, of course, entirely unlighted, and very badly charted; in the Dangerous Archipelago, through which we were fools enough to go, we were perfectly in ignorance of where we were for a whole night and half the next day, and this in the midst of invisible islands and rapid and variable currents; and we were lucky when we found our whereabouts at last. We have twice had all we wanted in the way of squalls; once, as I came on deck, I found the green sea over the cockpit coamings and running down the companion like a brook to meet me; at the same moment the foresail sheet jammed and the captain had no knife; this was the only occasion on the cruise that ever I set hand to a rope, but I worked like a Trojan, judging the possibility of haemorrhage better than the certainty of drowning. Another time I saw a rather singular thing: our whole ship's company as pale as paper from the captain to the

Princess Lilioukalani (sister of Kalakaua)

cook; we had a black squall astern on the port side and a white squall ahead to starboard; the complication passed off innocuous, the black squall only fetching us with its tail, and the white one slewing off somewhere else. Twice we were a long while (days) in the close vicinity of hurricane weather, but again luck prevailed, and we saw none of it. These are dangers incident to these seas and small craft. What was an amazement, and at the same time a powerful stroke of luck, both our masts were rotten, and we found out — I was going to say in time, but it was stranger and luckier than that. The head of the mainmast hung over so that hands were afraid to go to the helm; and less than three weeks before — I am not sure it was more than a fortnight — we had been nearly twelve hours beating off the lee shore of Eimeo (or Moorea, next island to Tahiti) in half a gale of wind with a violent head sea: she would neither tack nor wear once, and had to be boxed off with the mainsail — you can imagine what an ungodly show of kites we carried — yet the mast stood. The very day after that, in the southern bight of Tahiti, we had a near squeak, the wind suddenly coming calm; the reefs were close in with, my eye! what a surf! The pilot thought we were gone, and the captain had a boat cleared, when a lucky squall came to our rescue. My wife, hearing the order given about the boats, remarked to my mother: 'Isn't that nice? We shall soon be ashore.' Thus does the female mind unconsciously skirt along the verge of eternity. Our voyage up here was most disastrous ... we were in the midst of the hurricane season, when even the hopeful builder and owner of the yacht had pronounced these seas unfit for her ... we were quite given up for lost in Honolulu: people had ceased to speak to Belle [Stevenson's stepdaughter] about the *Casco*, as a deadly subject.

But the perils of the deep were part of the programme and though I am very glad to be done with them for a while and comfortably ashore, where a squall does not matter a snuff to anyone, I feel pretty sure I shall want to go to sea again ere long. The dreadful risk I took was financial and double-headed. First, I had to sink a lot of money in the cruise, and if I didn't get health, how was I to get it back? I have got health to a wonderful extent; and as I have the most interesting matter for my book, bar accidents, I ought to get all I have laid out and a profit. But, second (what I own I never considered till too late), there was the danger of collisions, of damages and heavy repairs, of disablement, towing, and salvage; indeed, the cruise might have turned round and cost me double. Nor will this danger be quite over till I hear the yacht is in San Francisco; for though I have shaken the dust of her deck from my feet, I fear (as a point of law) she is still mine till she gets there.

From my point of view, up to now the cruise has been a wonderful success. I never knew the world was so amusing. On the last voyage we had grown so used to sea-life that no one wearied, though it lasted a full month, except Fanny, who is always ill. All the time our visits to the islands have been more like dreams than realities: the people, the life, the beachcombers, the old stories and songs I have

Lloyd, Fanny, Louis and Margaret Stevenson entertain King Kalakaua aboard Casco

picked up, so interesting; the climate, the scenery, and (in some places) the women, so beautiful. The women are handsomest in Tahiti, the men in the Marquesas, both as fine types as can be imagined. Lloyd reminds me, I have not told you one characteristic incident of the cruise from a semi-naval point of view. One night we were going ashore in Anaho Bay; the most awful noise on deck; the breakers distinctly audible in the cabin; and there I had to sit below, entertaining in my best style a negroid native chieftain, much the worse for rum! You can imagine the evening's pleasure.

This naval report on cruising in the South Seas would be incomplete without one other trait. On our voyage up here I came one day into the dining-room, the hatch in the floor was open, the ship's boy was below with a baler, and two of the hands were carrying buckets as for a fire; this meant that the pumps had ceased working.

One stirring day was that in which we sighted Hawaii. . . . The swell the heaviest I have ever been out in — I tried in vain to estimate the height, *at least* fifteen feet — came tearing after us about a point and a half off the wind. We had the best hand — old Louis — at the wheel; and really, he did nobly, and had noble luck, for it never caught us once. At times it seemed we must have it; old Louis would look over his shoulder with the queerest look and dive down his neck into his shoulders; and then it missed us somehow, and only sprays came over our quarter. . . . I never remember anything more delightful and exciting. Pretty soon after we were lying absolutely becalmed under the lee of Hawaii, of which we had been warned: and the captain never confessed he had done it on purpose, but when accused, he smiled. Really, I supposed he did quite right, for we stood committed to a dangerous race, and to bring her to the wind would have been rather a heart-sickening manoeuvre.

R.L.S.

Letter to Charles Baxter
Honolulu, 8th March 1889

My dear Charles, — At last I have the accounts; the Doer has done excellently ... I have the retrospective horrors on me when I think of the liabilities I incurred; but, thank God, I think I'm in port again, and I have found one climate in which I can enjoy life. Even Honolulu is too cold for me; but the south isles were a heaven upon earth to a puir, catarrhal party like Johns'one. We think, as Tahiti is too complete a banishment, to try Madeira. It's only a week from England, good communications, and I suspect in climate and scenery not unlike our dear islands; in people, alas! there can be no comparison. But friends could go, and I could come in summer, so I should not be quite cut off.

Lloyd and I have finished a story, *The Wrong Box*. If it is not funny, I am sure I do not know what is. I have split over writing it. Since I have been here, I have been toiling like a galley slave. . . . This spasm of activity has been chequered with champagne parties: Happy and Glorious, Hawaii Ponoi paua; kuo moi — (Native Hawaiians, dote upon your monarch) Hawaiian God save the King. (In addition to my other labours, I am learning the language with a native moonshee.) Kalakaua is a terrible companion; a bottle of fizz is like a glass of sherry to him; he thinks nothing of five or six in an afternoon as a whet for dinner. You should see a photograph of our party after an afternoon with H.H.M.: my! what a crew! —Yours ever affectionately.

ROBERT LOUIS STEVENSON

Letter to Sidney Colvin
Honolulu, March 1889

My dear Colvin, — Still no word from you! I am utterly cast down; but I will try to return good for evil and for once give you news. We are here in the suburb of Honolulu in a rambling house or set of houses in a great garden. . . . The town is some three miles away, but the house is connected by telephone with the chief shops, and the tramway runs to within a quarter of a mile of us. I find Honolulu a beastly climate after Tahiti and have been in bed a little; but my colds *took on no catarrhal symptom*, which is staggeringly delightful. . . . Fanny is, I think, a good deal better on the whole, having profited like me by the tropics; my mother and Lloyd are first-rate. I do not think I have heard from you since last May; and this really frightens me. Do write, even now. Scribners Sons it should be; we shall probably be out of this some time in April, home some time in June. But the world whirls to me perceptibly, a mass of times and seasons and places and engagements, and seas to cross, and continents to traverse, so that I scarce know where I am. Well, I have had a brave time. . . . Is it possible I have wounded you in some way? I scarce like to dream that it is possible; and yet I know too well it may be so. If so, don't write, and you can pitch into me when we meet. I am, admittedly, as mild as London Stout now; and the Old Man Virulent much a creature of the past. My dear Colvin, I owe to you and Fleeming Jenkin, the two older men who took the trouble, and knew how to make a friend of me, everything I have or am: if I have behaved ill, just hold on and give me a chance, you shall have the slanging of me and I bet I shall prefer it to this silence. — Ever, my dear Colvin, your most affectionate

R.L.S.

Feast for the King and Princess of Hawaii

The Bush, Hawaii

My dear Friend, — Louis has improved so wonderfully in the delicious islands of the South Seas, that we think of trying yet one more voyage. We are a little uncertain as to how we shall go, whether in a missionary ship, or by hiring schooners from point to point, but the 'unregenerate' islands we must see. I suppose we shall be off some time in June, which will fetch us back to England in another year's time. You could hardly believe it if you could see Louis now. He looks as well as he ever did in his life, and has had no sign of cough or haemorrhage (begging pardon of Nemesis) for many months. It seems a pity to return to England until his health is firmly re-established, and also a pity not to see all that we can see quite easily starting from this place; and which will be our only opportunity in life. Of course there is the usual risk from hostile natives, and the horrible sea, but a positive risk is so much more wholesome than a negative one, and it is all such joy to Louis and Lloyd. As for me, I hate the sea, and am afraid of it (though no one will believe that because in time of danger I do not make an outcry — nevertheless I _am_ afraid of it, and it is not kind to me), but I love the tropic weather, and the wild people, and to see my two boys so happy. Mrs Stevenson is going back to Scotland in May, as she does not like to be longer away from her old sister, who has been very ill. And besides, we do not feel justified in taking her to the sort of places we intend to visit. As for me, I can get comfort out of very rough surroundings for my people, I can work hard and enjoy it. I can even shoot pretty well, and though I 'don't want to fight, by jingo if I must', why I can. I don't suppose there will be any occasion for that sort of thing — only in case.

I am not quite sure of the names, but I *think* our new cruise includes the Gilberts, the Fijis, and the Solomons. Louis will write the particulars. As for myself, I have more cares than I was really fit for. To keep house on a yacht is no easy thing. When Louis and I broke loose from the ship and lived alone amongst the natives, I got on very well. It was when I was deathly sick, and the question was put to me by the cook, 'What shall we have for the cabin dinner, what for tomorrow's breakfast, what for lunch? and what about the sailors' food? Please come and look at the biscuits, for the weevils have got into them, and show me how to make yeast that will rise of itself, and smell the pork which seems pretty high, and give me directions about making a pudding with molasses — and what is to be done about the bugs?' — etc., etc. In the midst of heavy dangerous weather, when I was lying on the floor clutching a basin, down comes the mate with a cracked head, and I must needs cut off the hair matted with blood, wash and dress the wound and administer restoratives. I do not like being 'the lady of the yacht', but ashore! O, then I felt I was repaid for all. I wonder did any of my letters from beautiful Tautira ever come to hand, with the descriptions of our life with Louis's adopted brother Ori a Ori? Ori wrote to us, if no one else did, and I mean to give you a translation of his letter. . . .

I find my head swimming so that I cannot write any more. I wish some rich Catholic would send a parlour organ to Pere Bruno of Tautira. I am going to try and save money to do it myself, but he may die before I have enough. I feel ashamed to be sitting here when I think of that old man who cannot draw because of scrivener's paralysis, who has no one year in and year out to speak to but natives (our Rui is a Protestant, not bigoted like the rest of them — but still a Protestant) and the only pastime he has is playing on an old broken parlour organ whose keys are mostly dumb. I know no more pathetic figure. Have you no rich Catholic friends who would send him an organ that he could play upon? Of course, I am talking nonsense, and yet I know somewhere that person exists if only I knew the place.

Our dearest love to you all.

FANNY

Letter to Henry James
Honolulu, March 1889

My dear James, — Yes — I own up — I am untrue to friendship and (what is less, but still considerable) to civilisation. I am not coming home for another year. There it is, cold and bald, and now you won't believe in me at all, and serve me right (says you) and the devil take me. But look here, and judge me tenderly. I have had more fun and pleasure in my life these past months than ever before, and more health than in any time in ten long years. And even here in Honolulu I have withered in the cold; and this precious deep is filled with islands, which we may still visit; and though the sea is a deathful place, I like to be there, and like squalls (when they are over); and to draw near to a new island, I cannot say how much I like. In short, I take another year of this sort of life, and mean to try to work down among the poisoned arrows, and mean (if it may be) to come back again when the thing is through, and converse with Henry James as heretofore. . . . My wife has just sent to Mrs Sitwell a translation of a letter I have had from my chief friend in this part of the world; go and see her, and get a hearing of it; it will do you good; it is a better method of correspondence than even Henry James's. I jest, but seriously it is a strange thing for a tough, sick, middle-aged scrivener like R.L.S. to receive a letter so conceived from a man fifty years old, a leading politician, a crack orator, and the great wit of his village; boldly say 'the highly popular M.P. of Tautira'. My nineteenth century strikes here, and lies alongside of something beautiful and ancient. I would rather have received it than written *Redgauntlet* or

Iolani Palace, Honolulu

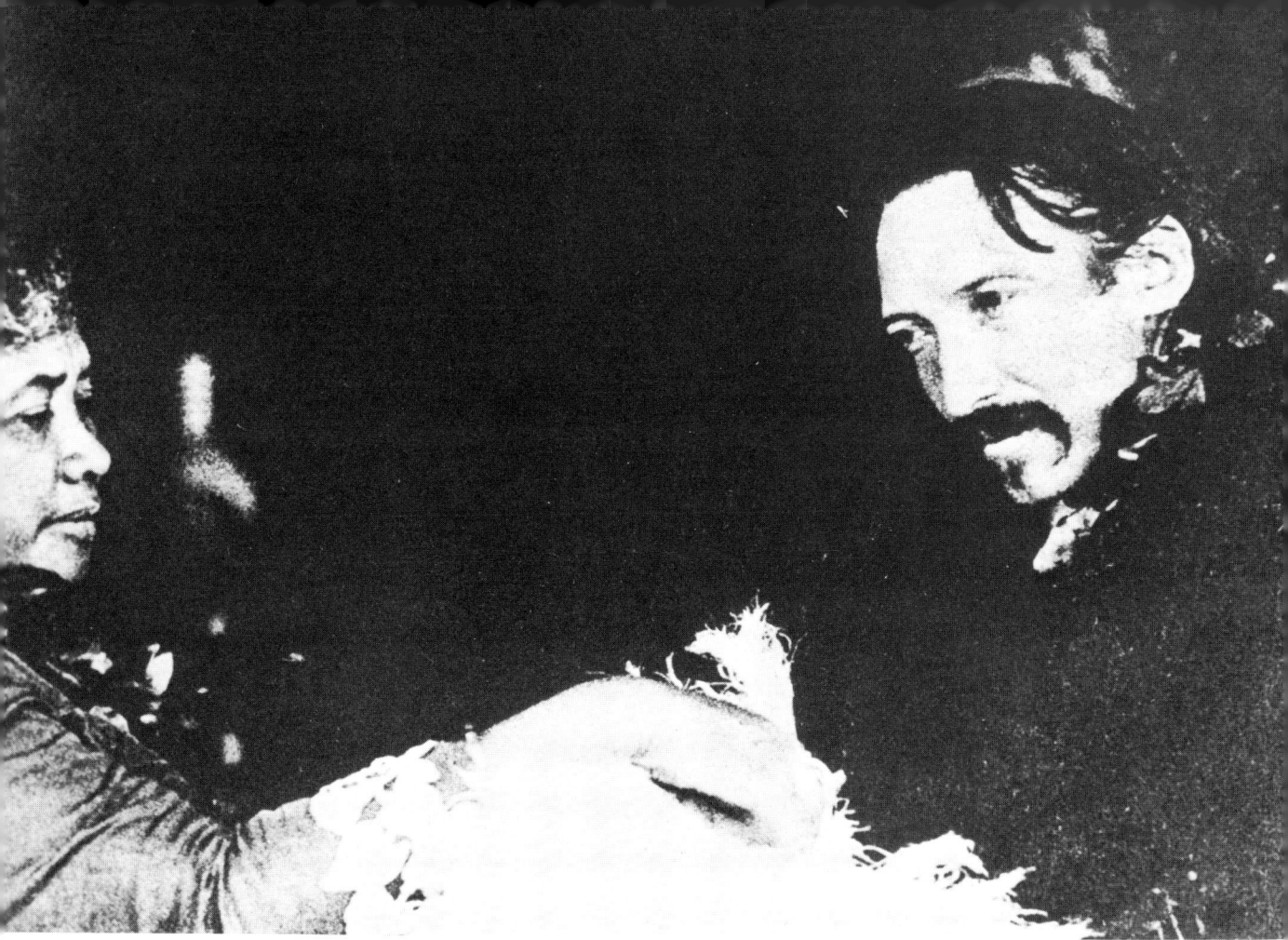

Stevenson with Princess Lilioukalani

the sixth *Aeneia*. All told, if my books have enabled or helped me to make this
voyage, to know Rui, and to have received such a letter, they have (in the old
prefatorial expression) not been writ in vain. It would seem from this that I have
been not so much humbled as puffed up; but, I assure you, I have in fact been
both. A little of what the letter says is my own earning; not all, but yet a little; and
the little makes me proud, and all the rest ashamed; and in the contrast, how
much more beautiful altogether is the ancient man than him of today!

Well, well, Henry James is pretty good, though he is of the nineteenth
century, and that glaringly. And to curry favour with him, I wish I could be more
explicit. . . . All are fairly well — the wife, your countrywoman, least of all;
troubles are not entirely wanting; but on the whole we prosper, and we are all
affectionately yours,

ROBERT LOUIS STEVENSON.

Letter to Sidney Colvin
Honolulu, April 2nd, 1889

My dear Colvin, — I am beginning to be ashamed of writing on to you without
the least acknowledgement, like a tramp; but I do not care — I am hardened; and

whatever be the cause of your silence, I mean to write till all is blue. I am outright ashamed of my news, which is that we are not coming home for another year. I cannot but hope it may continue the vast improvement of my health; I think it is good for Fanny and Lloyd; and we have all a taste for this wandering and dangerous life. My mother I send home, to my relief, as this part of our cruise will be (if we can carry it out) rather difficult in places . . . but if we can pull it off in safety, gives me a fine book of travel, and Lloyd a fine lecture and diorama, which should vastly better our finances.

I feel as if I were untrue to friendship; believe me, Colvin, when I look forward to this absence of another year, my conscience sinks at thought of the Monument; but I think you will pardon me if you consider how much this tropical weather mends my health. Remember me as I was at home, and think of me sea-bathing and walking about, as jolly as a sandboy: you will own the temptation is strong; and as the scheme, bar fatal accidents, is bound to pay into the bargain, sooner or later, it seems it would be madness to come home now, with an imperfect book, no illustrations to speak of, no diorama, and perhaps fall sick again by autumn. I do not think I delude myself when I say the tendency to catarrh has visibly diminished.

It is a singular thing that as I was packing up old papers ere I left Skerryvore, I came on the prophecies of a drunken Highland sibyl, when I was seventeen. She said I was to be very happy, to visit America, and *to be much upon the sea*. It seems as if it were coming true with a vengeance. Also, do you remember my strong, old, rooted belief that I shall die by drowning? I don't want that to come true, though it is an easy death; but it occurs to me oddly, with these long chances in front. I cannot say why I like the sea; no man is more cynically and constantly alive to its perils; I regard it as the highest form of gambling; and yet I love the sea as much as I hate gambling. Fine, clean emotions; a world all and always beautiful; air better than wine; interest unflagging; there is upon the whole no better life. — Yours ever,

R.L.S.

Letter to Miss Adelaide Boodle
Honolulu, April 6th, 1889

My dear Miss Boodle, — . . . The Sandwich Isles do not interest us very much; we live here, oppressed with civilisation, and look for good things in the future. But it would surprise you if you came out tonight from Honolulu (all shining with electric lights, and all in a bustle from the arrival of the mail, which is to carry you these lines) and crossed the long wooden causeway along the beach, and came out on the road through Kapiolani park, and seeing a gate in the palings, with a tub of goldfish by the wayside, entered casually in. The buildings stand in three groups by the edge of the beach, where an angry little spitfire sea continually spirts and thrashes with impotent irascibility, the big seas breaking further out on the reef.

The first is a small house, with a very large summer parlour, or *lanai*, as they call it here, roofed, but practically open. There you will find the lamps burning and the family sitting about the table, dinner just done; my mother, my wife, Lloyd, Belle, my wife's daughter, Austin her child, and tonight (by way of rarity) a guest. All about the walls our South Seas curiosities, war clubs, idols, pearl shells, stone axes, etc.; and the walls are only a small part of a *lanai*, the rest being glazed or latticed windows, or mere open space. You will see there no sign of the Squire, however. . . . The next group of buildings is ramshackle, and quite dark, and here is another door — all these places open from the outside — and you go in, and find photography, tubs of water, negatives steeping, a tap, and a chair and an ink-bottle, where my wife is supposed to write; round a little further, a third door, entering which you find a picture upon the easel and a table sticky with paints; . . . no sign of the Squire in all this. But right opposite the studio door you have observed a third little house . . . it is a grim little wooden shanty;

The Stevensons 'at home': Waikiki lanai *(cottage)*

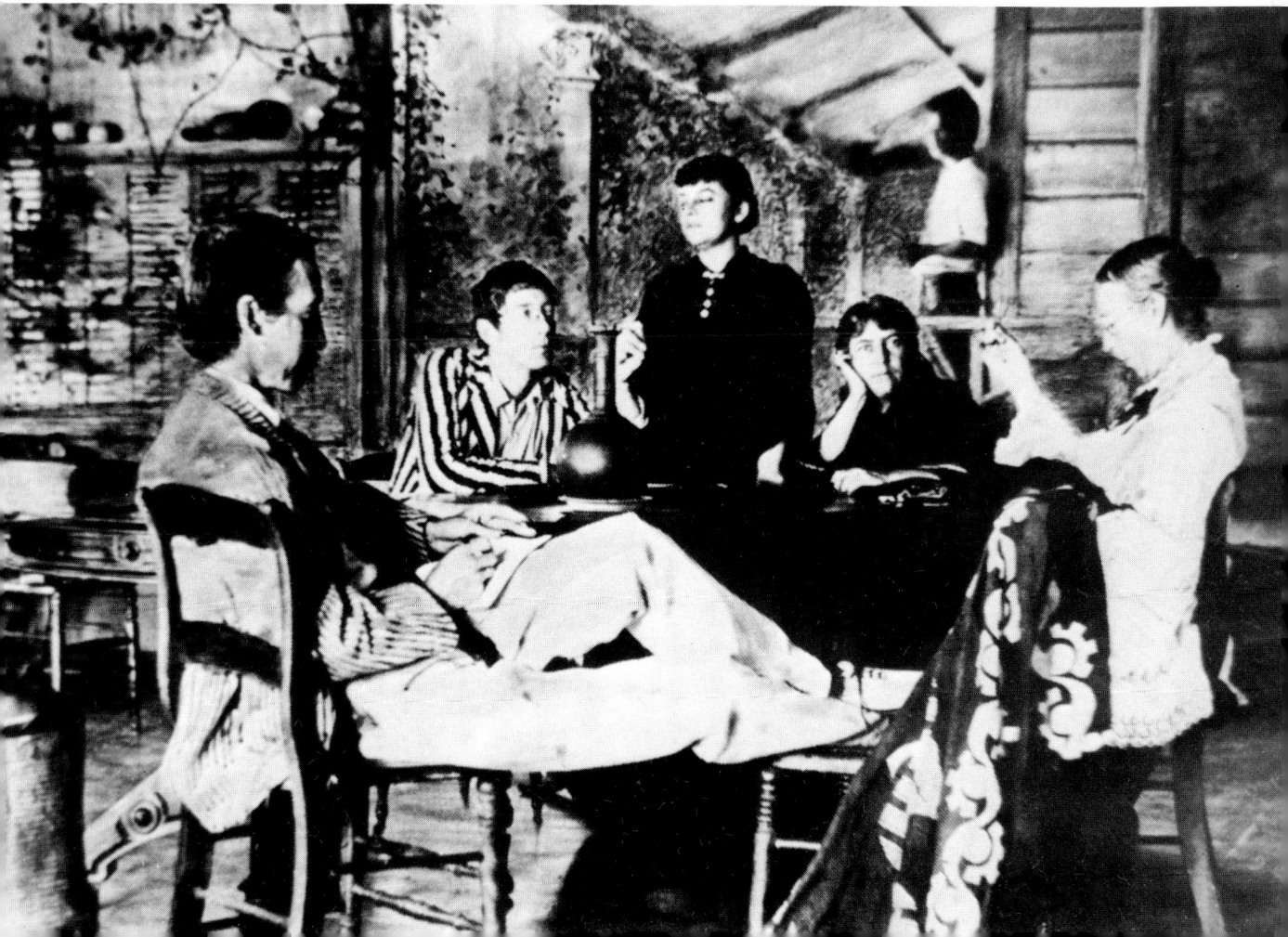

cobwebs bedeck it; friendly mice inhabit its recesses; the mailed cockroach walks upon the wall; so also, I regret to say, the scorpion. Herein are two pallet beds, two mosquito curtains, two tables laden with books and manuscripts, three chairs, and, in one of the beds, the Squire busy writing to yourself, as it chances, and just at this moment somewhat bitten by mosquitos. He has just set fire to the insect powder, and will be all right in no time; but just how he contemplates large white blisters, and would like to scratch them, but knows better. The house is not bare, walls pasted over with pages from the *Graphic*, *Harper's Weekly*, etc. The floor is matted, and I am bound to say the matting is filthy. There are two windows and two doors, one of which is condemned; on the panels of that last a sheet of paper is pinned up, and covered with writing. I cull a few plums: "A duck hammock for each person. A patent organ like the commandant's at Taillo hae. Cheap and bad cigars for presents. Revolvers. Permangate of potass. Liniment for the head and sulphur. Fine tooth-comb."

What do you think this is? Simply life in the South Seas foreshortened. These are a few of our desiderata for the next trip, which we jot down as they occur. . . . Tomorrow — think of it — I must be off by a quarter to eight to drive in to the palace and breakfast with his Hawaiian Majesty at 8.30: I shall be dead indeed. . . . To you we send all kinds of things, and I am the absentee Squire,

ROBERT LOUIS STEVENSON.

Stevenson at 39.

From An Intimate Portrait of RLS *by Lloyd Osbourne*

The seven months' cruise had had a marvellous effect on RLS. He had become almost well; could ride, take long walks, dine out, and in general lead the life of a man in ordinary health. Such climates were supposed to be harmful for tubercular patients, whom the local doctors sent away at once — but Stevenson throve. His fine complexion had regained its ruddy tint; his hair, now cut short, was no longer lank, but glossy and of a lighter brown; his eyes, always his most salient feature and always brilliant, had no longer that strange fire of disease: he walked with a firm, light step, and though to others he must have appeared thin and fragile, to us the transformation in him was astounding. In his soft white shirt, blue serge coat, white flannel trousers, white shoes and white yachting cap (such caps were his favourites till his death) he looked to perfection the famous author who had arrived in a yacht and who 'dressed the role' as the actors say, in a manner worthy of his dashing schooner.

It was typical of Stevenson that instead of choosing the best room in the house for his own, he should seek out a dilapidated, cobwebby little shack. . . . King Kalakaua would occasionally drop in on him for a long and confidential talk, while the horses of the royal equipage flicked their tails under a neighbouring tree, and the imposing coachman and footman dozed on their box. . . .

Sketch of R.L.S. 'famous author'

Stevenson and he became great friends, finding their strongest bond in Polynesian lore and antiquities. The king was a mine of information on these subjects. It was his hobby of hobbies to record the fast-fading history of his race and to pierce the mist in which so much of it was enveloped. Together they projected an excavation of the ancient royal tombs on Diamond Head, but at the last moment had to abandon it lest the king should play into the hands of his enemies and be accused of ransacking these graves for his personal profit . . . (Kalakaua) was always urging Stevenson to 'stay and make your home with us. Hawaii needs you'.

This home, wherever it was going to be, was causing Stevenson a good deal of concern. At first he anticipated returning to England; in fact for a while this was as good as settled; 'Skerryvore' (in Bournemouth) was still there temporarily rented, and absence, perhaps, was endowing it with a certain glamour. But most compelling of all, I think, was R.L.S.'s desire to stroll into the Savile Club and electrify his old friends as the returned seafarer from the South Sea Islands. At least he was constantly dwelling on this phase of his return, and choosing the exact hour when he could make the most dramatic entrance. But as the conviction grew that he never could be so well as in the Pacific, and with the vague and romantic idea of finding an island of his own, he began to talk of another cruise and look for the means.

The means, alas, were strictly limited to one ship, the missionary vessel, *Morning Star*, which in a few months' time was due to start on her annual tour of mission stations. Her itinerary was extraordinarily attractive; she went to many of the wildest and least-known islands of the Western Pacific; but her drawbacks were frightful — no smoking, not a drink, no profanity, church, nightly prayer meetings and an enforced intimacy with the most uncongenial of people. American missionaries often are excessively narrow, intolerant and puritanical; the prospect of four months in their society was calculated to make the stoutest hearts quail. . .   Our plans all seemed concentrated on the *Morning Star*, which was not due to sail for a long while; and it was with no sense of hurry or indecision that we remained on in Waikiki, one pleasant day merging into another in unbroken peace. But suddenly, out of a clear sky, we were thrown into a tremendous turmoil. One noonday R.L.S. came driving in from Honolulu, his horses in a lather, and it needed but a single look at his face to see that he was wildly excited.

'Have chartered a schooner!' he shouted out before he even jumped down; and as we all crowded about him, he breathlessly continued: 'Arranged the details and signed the charter-party as she was casting off — tug tooting, and people pulling at the owner's coat-tails, and the sweat running off our faces in a tin office! The *Equator*, sixty-eight tons, and due back from San Francisco in a month to pick us up for the Gilbert Islands. Finest little craft you ever saw in your life, and I have the right to take her anywhere at so much a day!'

The Pali, Hawaii

A hectic luncheon followed; champagne was opened in honour of the occasion, and we drank to the *Equator* in foaming bumpers; everybody talked at once amid an unimaginable hilarity, for were we not to sail away in a vessel of our own, and freed from the nightmare of the *Morning Star*?

'And we can smoke on that blessed ship!' cried Stevenson, with uplifted glass.

'And drink!' cried I. 'Hurrah for the *Equator*.'

'And swear!' exclaimed my mother delightedly — she who had never said 'damn' in her life.

. . . We looked out on one of the most inspiriting sights I have ever seen in my life — the *Equator* herself, under a towering spread of canvas, and as close in as her captain dared to put her, parting the blue water in flashes of spray on the way to San Francisco.

We were still watching when she broke out her ensign, and dipped it to us in farewell.

Our ship!

Letter to Charles Baxter
Honolulu, 10th May 1889

My dear Charles, — . . . This new cruise of ours is somewhat venturesome; and I think it needful to warn you not to be in a hurry to suppose us dead. In these ill-charted seas, it is quite on the cards we might be cast on some unvisited, or very rarely visited, island; that there we might lie for a long time, even years, unheard of; and yet turn up smiling at the hinder end. So do not let me be 'rowpit' till you get some certainty we have gone to Davie Jones in a squall, or graced the feast of some barbarian in the character of Long Pig.

I have just been a week away alone on the lee coast of Hawaii, the only white creature in many miles, riding five and a half hours one day, living with a native, seeing four lepers shipped off to Molokai, hearing native causes, and giving my opinion as *amicus curiae* as to the interpretation of a statue in English; a lovely week among God's best — at least God's sweetest works — Polynesians. It has bettered me greatly. If I could only stay there the time that remains, I could get my work done and be happy; but the care of my family keeps me in vile Honolulu, where I am always out of sorts, amidst heat and cold and cesspools and beastly *haoles*. What is a haole? You are one; and so, I am sorry to say, am I. [The Hawaiian name for white men.] After so long a dose of whites, it was a blessing to get among Polynesians again even for a week.

Well, Charles, there are waur haoles than yoursel', I'll say that for ye; and trust before I sail I shall get another letter with more about yourself. Ever your affectionate friend,

R.L.S.

Princess Kaiulani

Letter from R.L.S. to W. H. Low
Honolulu, (about) 20 May 1889

My dear Low, — . . . If you want to cease to be a republican, see my Kaiulani as she goes through —but she is gone already. You will die a red. I wear the colours of that little royal maiden, *Nous allons chanter à la ronde, si vous voulez*. Only she is not a blonde by several chalks, though she is but a half-blood and the wrong half Edinburgh Scots like mysel'. But, O, Low, I love the Polynesian: this civilisation of ours is a dingy, ungentlemanly business; it drops out too much of man, and too much of that the very beauty of the poor beast; who has his beauties in spite of Zola and Co. . . . But if you could live, the only white folk, in a Polynesian village; and drink that warm light *vin du pays* of human affection and enjoy that simple dignity of all about you — I will not gush, for I am now in my fortieth year, which seems highly unjust, but there it is, Mr Low, and the Lord enlighten your affectionate

R.L.S.

[Princess Kaiulani was born in Honolulu in 1875, daughter of Archibald S. Cleghorn from Edinburgh, who had married the sister of King Kalakaua, Princess Miriam Likelike. Kaiulani was the only child and heiress to the throne. Her mother died when she was twelve and she became a close friend of visitor R.L.S. whom her father had welcomed to his home in Honolulu. He called her his critic and said: 'If you like what I write, I know it is good.' In 1889, she was sent to boarding school in Britain to prepare her for her royal inheritance.]

To Princess Kaiulani (from *Ballads and Other Poems*)

> Forth from her land to mine she goes,
> The island maid, the island rose,
> Light of heart and bright of face:
> The daughter of a double race.
> Her islands here, in Southern Sun,
> Shall mourn their Ka'iulani gone,
> And I, in her dear banyan shade,
> Look vainly for my little maid.
>
> But our Scots islands far away
> Shall glitter with unwonted day,
> And cast for once their tempests by
> To smile in Ka'iulani's eye.

Written in April to Ka'iulani in the April of her age; and at Waikiki, within easy walk of Ka'iulani's banyan. When she comes to my land and her father's, and the

Princess Kaiulani, her father, A. G. Cleghorn and friend

rain beats upon the window (as I fear it will), let her look at this page; it will be like a weed gathered and pressed at home; and she will remember her own islands, and the shadow of the mighty tree; and she will hear the peacocks screaming in the dusk and the wind blowing in the palms; and she will think of her father sitting there alone. — R.L.S.

[Kaiulani returned to Hawaii in November 1897 her health shattered by Britain's climate. Stevenson was dead and she survived him by less than five years, dying in March 1899, aged 24. She lay in state dressed in white, on a purple velvet pall covered by the royal cloak of yellow feathers. Two crowns, one of white carnations, the other of the royal flower, yellow ilima, and the fragrant vine vaile, lay at her head.]

Letter from Fanny Stevenson to Sidney Colvin
Honolulu, May 21st, 1889

Best of Friends, — It was a joy inexpressible to get a word from you at last. . . . I wish you could have seen us both throwing over the immense package of letters searching for your handwriting. Now that we know you have been ill, please do let someone send us a line at our next address telling us how you are. What that next address may be we do not yet know, as our final movements are a little uncertain. To begin with, a trading schooner, the *Equator*, will come along some time in the first part of June, lie outside the harbour and signal to us. Within forty-eight hours we shall pack up our possessions, our barrel of sauer kraut, our barrel of salt onions, our bag of cocoanuts, our native garments, our tobacco, fish hooks, red combs and Turkey red calicoes (all the latter for trading purposes), our hand organ, photograph and painting materials, and finally our magic lantern — all these upon a large whaleboat. . . . Lloyd, also, takes a fiddle, a guitar, a native instrument, something like a banjo, called a taro-patch fiddle, and a lot of songbooks. We shall be carried first to one of the Gilberts, landing at Butaritari. The *Equator* is going about amongst the Gilbert group, and we have the right to keep her over when we like within reasonable limits. Finally she will leave us, and we shall have to take the chances of what happens next. We hope to see the Marshalls, the Carolines, the Fijis, Tonga and Samoa (also other islands that I do not remember), perhaps staying a little while in Sydney, and stopping on our way home to see our friends in Tahiti and the Marquesas.

I am very much exercised by one thing. Louis has the most enchanting material that anyone ever had in the whole world for his book, and I am afraid he is going to spoil it all. He has taken into his Scotch Stevenson head that a stern duty lies before him, and that his book must be a sort of scientific and historic impersonal thing, comparing the different languages (of which he knows nothing really) and the different peoples, the object being to settle the question as to

Princess Kaiulani with friends

whether they are of common Malay origin or not. Also to compare the Protestant and Catholic missions, etc., and the whole thing to be impersonal, leaving out all he knows of the people themselves. And I believe there is no one living who has got so near to them, or who understands them as he does. Think of a small treatise on the Polynesian races being offered to people who are dying to hear about Ori a Ori, the making of brothers with cannibals, the strange stories they told, and of the extraordinary adventures that befell us: suppose Herman Melville had given us his theories as to the Polynesian language and the probable good or evil results of the missionary influence instead of *Omoo* and *Typee.* . . . Louis says it is a stern sense of duty that is at the bottom of it, which is more alarming than anything else. I am so sure that you will agree with me that I am going to ask you to throw the weight of your influence as heavily as possible in the scales with me. Please refer to the matter in the letters we shall receive at our first stopping place, otherwise Louis will spend a great deal of time in Sydney actually reading other people's books on the islands. What a thing it is to have a 'man of genius' to deal with. It is like managing an overbred horse. Why with my own feeble hand I could write a book that the whole world would jump at. Please keep any letters of mine that contain any incidents of our wanderings. They are very exact as to facts, and Louis may, in this conscientious state of mind (indeed I am afraid he has), put nothing in his diary but statistics. Even if I thought it a desirable thing to write what he proposes, I should still think it impossible unless after we had lived and studied here some twenty years or more.

Now I am done with my complaining, and shall turn to the pleasanter paths. Louis went to one of the other islands a couple of weeks ago, quite alone, got drenched with rain and surf, rode over mountain paths — five and a half hours one day — and came back none the worse for it. Today he goes to Molokai, the leper island. He never has a sign of haemorrhage, the air cushion is a thing of the past, and altogether he is a new man. How he will do in the English climate again I do not know, but in these latitudes he is very nearly a well man, nothing seems to do him harm but overwork. That, of course, is sometimes difficult to prevent. Now, however, *The Master* is done, we have enough money to go upon and there is no need to work at all. I must stop. My dear love to you all.

FANNY V. DE G. STEVENSON

Letter to Fanny Stevenson
Kalawao, Molokai, May 1889

Dear Fanny, — I had a lovely sail up. Captain Cameron and Mr Gilfillan, both born in the States, yet the first still with a strong Highland, and the second still with a strong Lowland accent, were good company; the night was warm, the victuals plain but good. Mr Gilfillan gave me his berth, and I slept well, though I heard the sisters sick in the next stateroom, poor souls. Heavy rolling woke me in the morning; I turned in all standing, so went right on the upper deck. The day was on the peep out of a low morning bank, and we were wallowing along under stupendous cliffs. As the lights brightened, we could see certain abutments and buttresses on their front where wood clustered and grass grew brightly. But the whole brow seemed quite impassable, and my heart sank at the sight. Two thousand feet of rock making 19 degrees (the Captain guesses) seemed quite beyond my powers. However, I had come so far; and, to tell you the truth, I was so cowed with fear and disgust that I dared not go back on the adventure in the interests of my own self-respect. Presently we came up with the leper promontory, low-land, quite bare and bleak and harsh, a little town of wooden houses, two churches, a landing-stair, all unsightly, sour, northerly, lying athwart the sunrise, with the great wall of the pali cutting the world out on the south. Our lepers were sent on the first boat, about a dozen, one poor child very horrid, one white man, leaving a large grown family behind him in Honolulu, and then into the second boat stepped the sisters and myself. I do not know how it would have been with me had the sisters not been there. My horror of the horrible is about my weakest point; but the moral loveliness at my elbow blotted all else out; and when I found that one of them was crying, poor soul, quietly under her veil, I cried a little myself; then I felt as right as a trivet, only a little crushed to be there so uselessly. I thought it was a sin and a shame she should feel unhappy; I turned round to her, and said something like this: 'Ladies, God Himself is here to give you welcome. I'm sure it is good for me to be beside you; I hope it will be blessed to me; I thank you for myself and the good you do me.' It seemed to cheer her up; but indeed I had scarce said it when we were at the landing-stairs, and there was a great crowd, hundreds of (God save us) pantomime masks in poor human flesh, waiting to receive the sisters and the new patients.

Every hand was offered: I had gloves, but I had made up my mind on the boat's voyage *not* to give my hand; that seemed less offensive than the gloves. So the sisters and I went up among that crew, and presently I got aside (for I felt I had no business there) and set off on foot across the promontory, carrying my wrap and the camera. All horror was quite gone from me; to see these dread creatures smile and look happy was beautiful. On my way through Kalaupapa I was exchanging cheerful *alohas* with the patients coming galloping over on their horses; I was stopping to gossip at house-doors; I was happy, only ashamed of myself that I was here for no good. One woman was pretty, and spoke good English, and was infinitely engaging and (in the old phrase) towardly; she thought I was the new white patient; and when she found I was only a visitor, a curious change came into her face and voice — the only sad thing, morally, sad, I mean — that I met that morning. But for all that, they tell me none want to leave. Beyond Kalaupapa the houses become rare; drystone dykes, grassy, stony land, one sick pandanus; a dreary country, from overhead in the little clinging wood shogs of the pali chirruping of birds fell; the low sun was right in my face; the trade blew pure and cool and delicious; I felt as right as ninepence, and stopped and chatted with the patients whom I still met on their horses, with not the least disgust. About halfway over, I met the superintendent (a leper) with a horse for me, and O, wasn't I glad! But the horse was one of those curious, dogged cranky brutes that always dully want to go somewhere else, and my traffic with him completed my crushing fatigue. I got to the guest-house, an empty house with several rooms, kitchen, bath, etc. There was no one there, and I let the horse go loose in the garden, lay down on the bed and fell asleep.

Dr Swift woke me and gave me breakfast, then I came back and slept again while he was at the dispensary, and he woke me for dinner; and I came back and slept again, and he woke me about six for supper; and then in about an hour I felt tired again, and came up to my solitary guest-house, played the flageolet, and am now writing to you. As yet, you see, I have seen nothing of the settlement, and my crushing fatigue (though I believe that was moral and a measure of my cowardice) and the doctor's opinion make me think the pali hopeless. 'You don't look a strong man,' said the doctor; 'but are you sound?' I told him the truth; then he said it was out of the question, and if I were to get up at all, I must be carried up. But, as it seems, men as well as horses continually fall on this ascent: the doctor goes up with a change of clothes — it is plain that to be carried would in itself be very fatiguing to both mind and body; and I should then be at the beginning of thirteen miles of mountain road to be ridden against time. How should I come through? I hope you will think me right in my decision: I mean to stay, and shall not be back in Honolulu till Saturday, June first.

Dr Swift has a wife and infant son, beginning to toddle and run, and they live here as composed as brick and mortar — at least the wife does, a Kentucky German, a fine enough creature, I believe, who was quite amazed at the sisters shedding tears! How strange is mankind! Gilfillan too, a good fellow I think, and far from stupid, kept up his hard Lowland Scottish talk in the boat while the sister was covering her face; but I believe he knew, and did it (partly) in embarrassment and part perhaps in mistaken kindness. And that was one reason, too, why I made my speech to them. Partly, too, I did it because I was ashamed to do so, and remembered one of my golden rules, 'When you are shamed to speak, speak up at once'. But, mind you, that rule is only golden with strangers; with your own folk, there are other considerations. This is a strange place to be in. A bell has sounded at intervals while I wrote, now all is still but a musical humming of the sea, not unlike the sound of the telegraph wires; the night is quite cool and pitch dark, with a small fine rain; one light over in the leper settlement, one cricket whistling in the garden, my lamp here by my bedside, and my pen cheeping between my inky fingers.

Next day, lovely morning, slept all night, 80 degrees in the shade, strong, sweet Anaho trade-wind.

LOUIS

The Stevensons at cards

Letter to Sidney Colvin
Honolulu, June 1889

My dear Colvin, — I am just home after twelve days' journey to Molokai, seven of them at the leper settlement, where I can only say that the sight of so much courage, cheerfulness, and devotion stung me too high to mind the infinite pity and horror of the sights. I used to ride over from Kalawao to Kalaupapa (about three miles across the promontory, the cliff-wall, ivied with forest and yet inaccessible from steepness, on my left), go to the Sisters' home, which is a miracle of neatness, play a game of croquet with seven leper girls (90 degrees in the shade), get an old-maid meal served me by the sisters, and ride home again, tired enough, but not too tired. The girls all have dolls, and love dressing them. You who know so many dressmakers, please make it known it would be an acceptable gift to send scraps for doll dressmaking to the Reverend Sister Maryanne. . . .

I have seen sights that cannot be told, and heard stories that cannot be repeated: yet I never admired my poor race so much, nor (strange as it may seem) loved life more than in the settlement. A horror of moral beauty broods over the place: that's like bad Victor Hugo, but it is the only way I can express the sense that lived with me all these days. And this even though it was in great part Catholic, and my sympathies flew never with so much difficulty as towards Catholic virtues. The passbook kept with heaven stirs me to anger and laughter. One of the sisters calls the place 'the ticket office to heaven'. Well, what is the odds? They do their darg, and do it with kindness and efficiency incredible; and we must take folk's virtues as we find them, and love the better part. Of old Damien, whose weaknesses and worse perhaps I heard fully, I think only the more. It was a European peasant: dirty, bigoted, untruthful, unwise, tricky, but superb with generosity, residual candour and fundamental good-humour: convince him he had done wrong (it might take hours of insult) and he would undo what he had done and like his corrector better. A man, with all the grime and patriness of mankind, but a saint and hero all the more for that.

The place as regards scenery is grand, gloomy and bleak . . . the low, bare, stony promontory edged in between the cliff and the ocean, two little towns (Kalawao and Kalaupapa) seated on either side of it, as bare almost as bathing machines upon a beach; and the population — gorgons and chimaeras dire. All this tear of the nerves I bore admirably; and the day after I got away, rode twenty miles along the opposite coast and up into the mountains; . . . and I was riding the day after, so I need say no more about health. Honolulu does not agree with me at all: I am always out of sorts there, with slight headache, blood to the head, etc. I had a good deal of work to do and did it with miserable difficulty; and yet all the time I have been gaining strength, as you see, which is highly encouraging. By the time I am done with this cruise I shall have the material for a very singular book of travels: names of strange stories and characters; so generous a farrago. I am going down now to get the story of a shipwrecked family who were fifteen months on an island with a murderer: there is a specimen. The Pacific is a strange place; the nineteenth century only exists there in spots; all round, it is a no-mans land of the ages, a stir-about of epochs and races, barbarisms and civilisations, virtues and crimes.

It is good of you to let me stay longer, but if I had known how ill you were, I should be now on my way home. I had chartered my schooner and made all arrangements before (at last) we got definite news. I feel highly guilty; I should be back to insult and worry you a little. . . . Yours ever,

R.L.S.

The leper settlement, Molokai

In the South Seas — The Eight Islands: The Kona Coast

... It was on a Saturday afternoon that the steamer conveyed me to Hookena. She was charged with tourists on their way to the volcano; and I found it hard to justify my choice of a week in an unheard-of hamlet, rather than a visit to one of the admitted marvels of the world. ... On other islands I had been the centre of attention; here none observed my presence. One hundred and ten years before, the ancestors of these indifferents had looked in the faces of Cook and his seamen with admiration and alarm, called them gods, called them volcanoes; took their clothes for a loose skin, confounded their hats and their heads, and described their pockets as a 'treasure door, through which they plunge their hands into their bodies and bring forth cutlery and necklaces and cloth and nails', and today the coming of the most attractive stranger failed (it would appear) to divert them from Miss Porter's *Scottish Chiefs*: for that was the novel of the day. ...

Letter to James Payn
[Met in his days of writing for Cornhill Magazine]
Honolulu, H.I., June 13th, 1889

My dear James Payn, — I get sad news of you here at my offsetting for further voyages: I wish I could say what I feel. Sure there was never any man less deserved this calamity; for I have heard you speak time and again, and I remember nothing that was unkind, nothing that was untrue, nothing that was not helpful from your lips. It is the ill-talkers that should hear no more. God knows, I know no word of consolation; but I do feel your trouble. You are the more open to letters now; let me talk to you for two pages. I have nothing but happiness to tell; and you may bless God you are a man so sound-hearted that (even in the freshness of your calamity) I can come to you with my own good fortune unashamed and secure of sympathy. It is a good thing to be a good man, whether deaf or whether dumb; and all of our fellow-craftsmen (whom yet they count a jealous race), I never knew one but gave you the name of honesty and kindness: come to think of it gravely, this is better than the finest hearing. We are all on the march to deafness, blindness, and all conceivable and fatal disabilities; we shall not all get there with

Father Damien with leper children

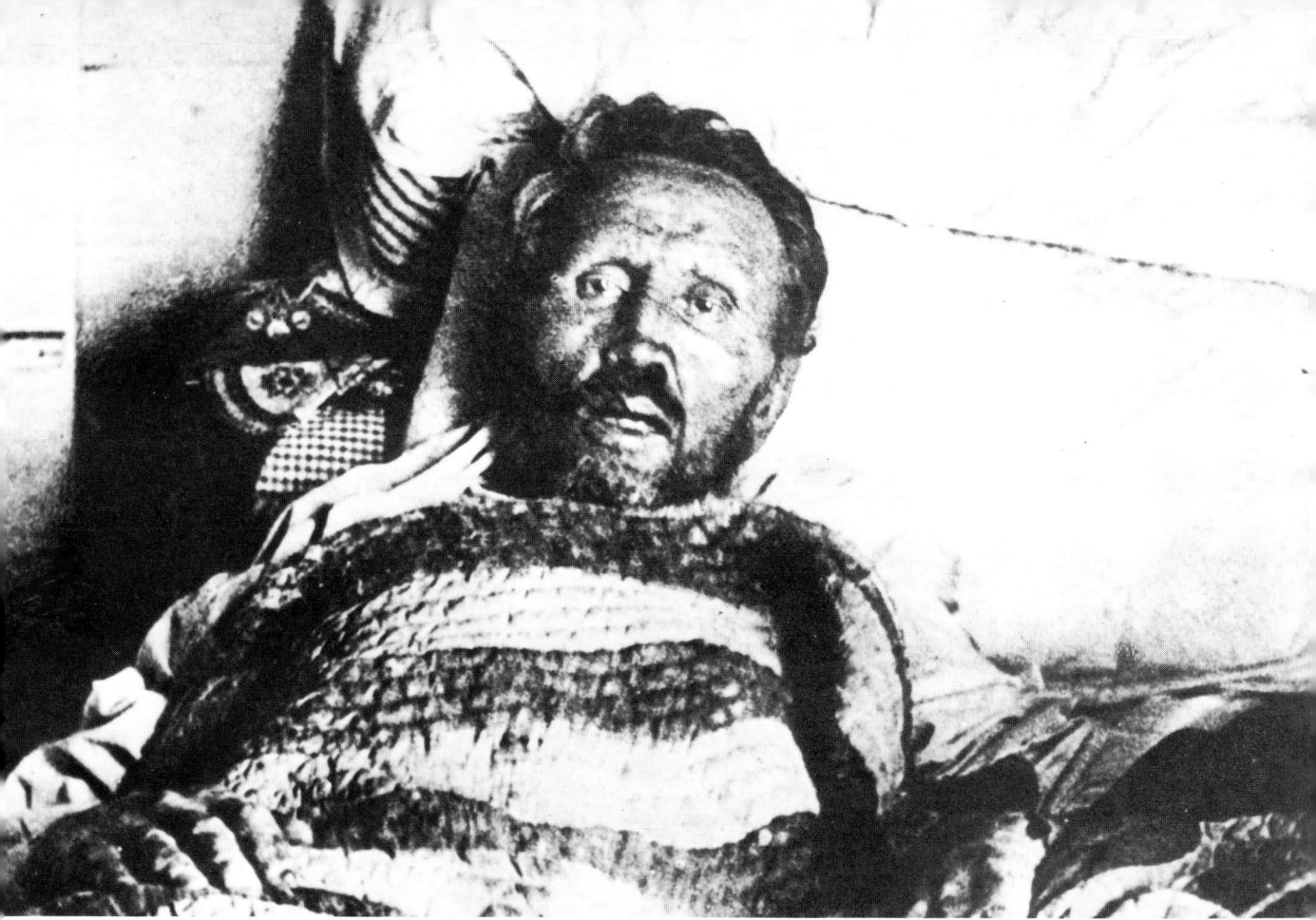

Damien on deathbed

a report so good. My good news is a health astonishingly reinstated. This climate; these voyagings; these landfalls at dawn; new islands peaking from the morning bank; new forested harbours; new passing alarms of squalls and surf; new interests of gentle natives — the whole tale of my life is better to me than any poem.

I am fresh just now from the leper settlement of Molokai, playing croquet with seven leper girls, sitting and yarning with old, blind, leper beachcombers in the hospital, sickened with the spectacle of abhorrent suffering and deformation amongst the patients, touched to the heart by the sight of lovely and effective virtues in their helpers, no stranger time have I ever had, nor any so moving. I do not think it a little thing to be deaf, God knows, and God defend me from the same! — but to be a leper, or one of the self-condemned, how much more awful! and yet there's a way there also. 'There are Molokais everywhere,' said Mr Dutton, Father Damien's dresser; you are but new landed in yours; and my dear and kind adviser, I wish you, with all my soul, that patience and courage which you will require. . . .

Yours affectionately (although so near a stranger),

ROBERT LOUIS STEVENSON

Letter to Mrs Thomas Stevenson
Honolulu, June 1889

My dear Mother, — . . . I was a week in the leper settlement, hag-ridden by horrid sights but really inspired with the sight of so much goodness in the helpless and so much courage and unconsciousness in the sick. The Bishop Home (the Sisters' place) is perfect; I went there most days to play croquet with seven little lepers, and the thermometer sometimes ninety in the shade. . . . The girls enjoyed the game a good deal, and the honour and glory of a clean Laole gentleman for playmate yet more. They were none of them badly disfigured, but some of the bystanders were dreadful; but indeed I have seen sights to turn any man's hair white. The croquet helped me a bit, as I felt I was not quite doing nothing; Sister Maryanne wanted me to sit down the second day, and only tell the girls; I said, 'They would not enjoy that' — 'Ah,' said she, with a smiling eye, 'you say that, but the truth is you enjoy playing yourself!' And so I did. When I came on board the *Mokolii* (little 40-ton steamer) to leave, I had no proper pass and was refused entrance. I saw some very remarkable fireworks, I can tell you, for I had had enough and to spare of the distressful country. But it was all made right; the captain took me ashore the same evening at the north end of the island, gave me a mount, introduced me to an innumerable Irish family where I had supper and a bed, and gave me a horse and a mounted guide next day, with whom I rode twenty miles to Mr Meyer's house. The next day I had another ride, a mighty rough drive over a kind of road to the landing place; caught the *Mokolii* again, and was in Honolulu the morning after about nine, very sunburnt and rudely well. How is that for activity and rustic strength?

Grace is not invariable but (I may say) frequent; and when not forgotten is (ahem!) very well said. Joe, Lloyd and I are getting up music; guitar, taropatch, flageolet and voice for the show. Le bon Damien is to give us a choice of his comic slides; he has given us already a complete set of the life of Christ; we have a fine magic lantern. . . . Ah Foo is death on Damien, but indeed we all exceedingly like him; he reminds us of Colvin in many ways, which you know is a big word for us. . . .

Was at a school examination yesterday (girls' school); it is a plain-looking race; more pretty girls in the little box at Tautira than in all this big hall; but they sang, and recited, and played the piano, like any European school and for the singing (and the recitation too) far away better. Must dry up. Much love. — Ever afft. son,

R.L.S.

PART TWO

SECOND VOYAGE
June to December 1889

In the trading schoon *Equator*, from Honolulu, the Hawaiian capital, where Stevenson had stayed in the interval, to the Gilberts and thence to Samoa.

Schooner Equator

Passengers and crew on Equator

PART TWO

News item from *Honolulu Pacific Advertiser*
24 June 1889

Robert Louis Stevenson and party leave today by the schooner *Equator* for the Gilbert Islands. . . . It is to be hoped that Mr Stevenson will not fall victim to native spears; but in his present state of bodily health, perhaps the temptation to kill him may not be very strong.

In the South Seas: The Gilberts — Butaritari

At Honolulu we said farewell to the *Casco* and to Captain Otis, and our next adventure was made in changed conditions. Passage was taken for myself, my wife, Mr Osbourne, and my China boy, Ah Fu, on a pigmy trading schooner, the *Equator*, Captain Dennis Reid; and on a certain bright June day in 1889, adorned in the Hawaiian fashion with the garlands of departure, we drew out of port and bore with a fair wind for Micronesia.

The whole extent of the South Seas is a desert of ships; more especially that part where we were now to sail. No post runs in these islands; communication is by accident; where you may have designed to go is one thing, where you shall be able to arrive, another. It was my hope, for instance, to have reached the Carolines, and returned to the light of day by way of Manila and the China ports; and it was in Samoa that we destined to reappear and be once more refreshed with the sight of mountains. Since the sunset faded from the peaks of Oahu six months had intervened, and we had seen no spot of earth so high as an ordinary cottage. Our path had been still on the flat sea, our dwellings upon unerected coral, our diet from the pickle-tub or out of tins; I had learned to welcome shark's flesh for a variety; and a mountain, an onion, an Irish potato or a beefsteak, had been long lost to sense and dear to aspiration.

The two chief places of our stay, Butaritari and Apemama, lie near the line; the latter within thirty miles. Both enjoy a superb ocean climate, days of blinding sun and bracing wind, nights of a heavenly brightness . . . they show the customary features of an atoll; the low horizon, the expanse of the lagoon, the sedge-like rim of palm-tops, the sameness and smallness of the land, the hugely superior size and interest of sea and sky. Life on such islands is in many points like life on shipboard. The atoll, like the ship, is soon taken for granted; and the islanders, like the ship's crew, become soon the centre of attention. The isles are populous, independent, seats of kinglets, recently civilised, little visited. In the last decade many changes have crept in; women no longer go unclothed till marriage; the widow no longer sleeps at night and goes abroad by day with the skull of her dead husband; and, firearms being introduced, the spear and the shark-tooth sword are sold for curiosities. Ten years ago all these things and practises were to be seen in use; yet ten years more, and the old society will have entirely vanished. We came in a happy moment to see its institutions still erect and (in Apemama) scare decayed. . . .

131

Populous and independent — warrens of men, ruled over with some rustic pomp — such was the first and still the recurring impression of these tiny lands. As we stood across the lagoon for the town of Butaritari, a stretch of the low shore was seen to be crowded with the brown roofs of houses; those of the palace and the king's summer parlour (which was of corrugated iron) glittered near one end conspicuously bright; the royal colours flew hard by on a tall flagstaff; in front, on an artificial islet, the gaol played the part of a martello. Even upon this first and distant view, the place had scarce the air of what it truly was, a village; rather of that which it was also, a pretty metropolis, a city rustic and yet royal. . . .

We may thus be said to have taken Butaritari by surprise. A few inhabitants were still abroad in the north end, at which we landed. As we advanced, we were soon done with encounter, and seemed to explore a city of the dead. Only, between the posts of open houses, we could see the townsfolk stretched in the siesta, sometimes a family together veiled in a mosquito net, sometimes a single sleeper on a platform like a corpse on a bier. . . .

It was now some while since we had met any but slumberers; and when we had wandered down the pier and stumbled at last into this bright shed, we were surprised to find it occupied by a society of wakeful people, some twenty souls in all, the court and guardsmen of Butaritari. The court ladies were busy making mats; the guardsmen yawned and sprawled. Half a dozen rifles lay on a rock and a cutlass was leaned against a pillar; the armoury of these drowsy musketeers. At the far end, a little closed house of wood displayed some tinsel curtains, and proved, upon examination, to be a privy on the European model. In front of this, upon some mats, lolled Tebureimoa, the king; beside him, on the panels of the house, two crossed rifles represented fasces. He wore pyjamas which sorrowfully misbecame his bulk; his nose was hooked and cruel, his body overcome with sodden corpulence, his eye timorous and dull; he seemed at once oppressed with drowsiness and held awake by apprehension; a pepper rajah muddled with opium, and listening for the march of a Dutch army, looks perhaps not otherwise. We were to grow better acquainted, and first and last I had the same impression; he seemed always drowsy, yet always to hearken and start; and, whether from remorse or fear, there is no doubt he seeks a refuge in the abuse of drugs.

The rajah displayed no sign of interest in our coming. But the queen, who sat beside him in a purple sacque, was more accessible; and there was present an interpreter so willing that his volubility became at last the cause of our departure. He greeted us upon our entrance:

'That is the honourable King, and I am his interpreter,' he had said, with more stateliness than truth. For he held no appointment in the court, seemed extremely ill-acquainted with the island language, and was present, like ourselves, upon a visit of civility. Mr Williams was his name; an American darkey, runaway ship's cook, and barkeeper at *The Land We Live In* tavern, Butaritari. I never knew a man who had more words in his command or less truth to communicate; neither the gloom of the monarch, nor my own efforts to be distant,

Maniap of Tembinok's harem

could in the least abash him; and when the scene closed, the darkey ws left talking.

The town still slumbered, or had but just begun to turn and stretch itself; it was still plunged in heat and silence. So much the more vivid was the impression that we carried away of the house upon the islet, the Micronesian Saul wakeful amid his guards, and his unmelodious David, Mr Williams, chattering through the drowsy hours.

The Four Brothers

On the death of King Tetimararoa, Tebureimoa's father, Nakaeia, the eldest son, succeeded. He was a fellow of huge physical strength, masterful, violent, with a certain barbaric thrust and some intelligence of men and business. Alone in his islands, it was he who dealt and profited; he was the planter and the merchant; and his subjects toiled for his behoof in servitude. When they wrought long and well their taskmaster declared a holiday, and supplied and shared a general debauch. The scale of his providing was at times magnificent; six hundred dollars' worth of gin and brandy was set forth at once; the narrow land resounded with the noise of revelry; and it was a common thing to see the subjects (staggering themselves) parade their drunken sovereign on the forehatch of a wrecked vessel, king and commons howling and singing as they went. At a word from Nakaeia's mouth the revel ended; Makin became once more an isle of slaves and of

133

teetotallers; and on the morrow all the population must be on the roads or in the taro-patches toiling under his bloodshot eye.

The fear of Nakaeia filled the land. No regularity of justice was affected; there was no trial, there were no officers of the law; it seems there was but one penalty, the capital; and daylight assault and midnight murder were the forms of process. The king himself would play the executioner; and his blows were dealt by stealth, and with the help and countenance of none but his own wives. These were his oarswomen; one that caught a crab, he slew incontinently with the tiller; thus disciplined, they pulled him by night to the scene of his vengeance, which he would then execute alone and return well pleased with his connubial crew. The inmates of the harem held a station hard for us to conceive. Beasts of draught, and driven by the fear of death, they were yet implicitly trusted with their sovereign's life; they were still wives and queens, and it was supposed that no man should behold their faces. They killed by the sight like basilisks; a chance view of one of those boatwomen was a crime to be wiped out with blood.

In the days of Nakaeia the palace was beset with some tall cocoa-palms which commanded the enclosure. It chanced one evening, while Nakaeia sat below at supper with his wives, that the owner of the grove was in a treetop drawing palm-tree wine; it chanced that he looked down, and the king at the same moment looking up, their eyes encountered. Instant flight preserved the involuntary criminal. But during the remainder of that reign he must lurk and be hid by friends in remote parts of the isle; Nakaeia hunted him without remission, although still in vain; and the palms, accessories to the fact, were ruthlessly cut down. Such was the ideal of wifely purity in an isle where nubile virgins went naked as in paradise. And yet scandal found its way into Nakaeia's well-guarded harem. He was at that time the owner of a schooner, which he used for a pleasure-house, lodging on board as she lay anchored; and thither one day he summoned a new wife. She was one that had been sealed to him; that is to say (I presume), that he was married to her sister, for the husband of an elder sister has the call of the cadets. She was to be arrayed for the occasion; she would come scented, garlanded, decked with fine mats and family jewels, for marriage, as her friends supposed; for death, as she well knew. 'Tell me the man's name, and I will spare you,' said Nakaeia. But the girl was staunch; she held her peace, saved her lover; and the queens strangled her between the mats.

Nakaeia was feared; it does not appear that he was hated. Deeds that smell to us of murder wore to his subjects the reverent face of justice; his orgies made him popular; natives to this day recall with respect the firmness of his government; and even the whites, whom he long opposed and kept at arm's length, give him the name (in the canonical South Sea phrase) of 'a perfect gentleman when sober'.

When he came to lie, without issue, on the bed of death, he summoned his next brother, Nanteitei, made him a discourse on royal policy, and warned him he was too weak to reign. The warning was taken to heart, and for some while the government moved on the model of Nakaeia's. Nanteitei dispensed with guards and walked abroad alone with a revolver in a leather mailbag. To conceal his weakness he affected a rude silence; you might talk to him all day; advice, reproof, appeal, and menace alike remained unanswered. The number of his wives was seventeen, many of them heiresses; for the royal house is poor, and marriage was in these days a chief means of buttressing the throne. Nakaeia kept his harem busy for himself; Nanteitei hired it out to others. In his days, for instance, Messrs. Wightman built a pier with a verandah at the north end of the town. The masonry was the work of the seventeen queens, who toiled and waded there like fisher lasses; but the man who was to do the roofing durst not begin till they had finished, lest by chance he should look down and see them.

It was perhaps the last appearance of the harem gang. For some time already Hawaiian missionaries had been seated at Butaritari — Maka and Kanoa, two brave childlike men. Nakaeia would have none of their doctrine; he was perhaps jealous of their presence; being human, he had some affection for the persons. In the house, before the eyes of Kanoa, he slew with his own hand three sailors of Oahu, crouching on their backs to knife them, and menacing the missionary if he interfered; yet he not only spared him at the moment, but recalled him afterwards (when he had fled) with some expressions of respect. Nanteitei, the weaker man, fell more completely under the spell. Maka, a lighthearted, lovable, yet in his own trade very rigorous man — gained and improved an influence on the king which

Fanny and Louis Stevenson with Nan Tok' and Nei Takauti

Island Speak House: Interior and Exterior

soon grew paramount. Nanteitei, with the royal house, was publicly converted; and, with a severity which liberal missionaries disavow, the harem was at once reduced. It was a compendium act. The throne was thus impoverished, its influence shaken, the queens' relatives mortified, and sixteen chief women (some of them great possessions) cast in a body on the market. I have been shipmates with a Hawaiian sailor who was successively married to two of these *impromptu* widows, and successively divorced by both for misconduct. That two great and rich ladies (for both of these were rich) should have married 'a man from another island' marks the dissolution of society. The laws besides were wholly remodelled, not always for the better. I love Maka as a man; as a legislator he has two defects: weak in the punishment of crime, stern to repress innocent pleasures.

War and revolution are the common successors of reform; yet Nanteitei died (of an overdose of chloroform) in quiet possession of the throne, and it was in the reign of the third brother, Nabakatokai, a man brave in body and feeble of character, that the storm burst. About this period, in almost every part of the group, the kings were murdered . . . Nabakatokai was more fortunate, his life and the royal style were spared him, but he was stripped of power. . . . He died some months before my arrival in the islands and no one regretted him; rather all looked hopefully to his successor. This was by repute the hero of the family. Alone of the four brothers, he had issue, a grown son, Natiata, and a daughter three years old. Natemat', *Mr Corpse*, was his appalling nickname, and he had earned it well. Again and again, at the command of Nakaeia, he had surrounded houses in the dead of night, cut down the mosquito bars and butchered families . . . he was installed, he proved a puppet and a trembler, the unwieldy shuttlecock of orators; and the reader has seen the remains of him in his summer parlour under the name of Tebureimoa.

The change in the man's character was much commented on in the island, and variously explained by opium and Christianity. To my eyes, there seemed no change at all, rather an extreme consistency. Mr Corpse was afraid of his brother; King Tebureimoa is afraid of the Old Men. Terror of the first nerved him for deeds of desperation; fear of the second disables him for the least act of government. He played his part of bravo in the past, following the line of least resistance, butchering others in his own defence: today, grown elderly and heavy, a convert, a reader of the Bible, perhaps a penitent, conscious at least of accumulated hatreds, and his memory charged with images of violence and blood, he capitulates to the Old Men, fuddles himself with opium, and sits among his guards in dreadful expectation. The same cowardice that put into his hand the knife of the assassin deprives him of the sceptre of a king. . . .

The justice of facts is strange, and strangely just; Nakaeia, the author of these deeds, died at peace discoursing on the craft of kings; his tool suffers daily death for his enforced complicity. Not the nature, but the congruity of men's deeds and circumstances damn and save them; and Tebureimoa from the first has been incongruously placed. At home, in a quiet by-street of a village, the man had been a worthy carpenter, and, even bedevilled as he is, he shows some private virtues. He has no lands, only the use of such as are impignorate for fines, he cannot enrich himself in the old way by marriages; thrift is the chief pillar of his future, and he knows and uses it. Eleven foreign traders pay him a patent of a hundred dollars, some two thousand subjects pay capitation at the rate of a dollar for a man, half a dollar for a woman, and a shilling for a child: allowing for the exchange, perhaps a total of three hundred pounds a year. He had been some nine months on the throne: had bought his wife a silk dress and hat, figure unknown, and himself a uniform at three hundred dollars; had sent his brother's photograph to be enlarged in San Francisco at two hundred and fifty dollars; had greatly reduced that brother's legacy of debt; and had still sovereigns in his pocket. An affectionate brother, a good economist; he was besides a handy carpenter, and cobbled occasionally on the woodwork of the palace. It is not wonderful that Mr Corpse has virtues; that Tebureimoa should have a diversion filled me with surprise.

Around our house

The men are of a marked Arabian cast of features, often bearded and mustached, often gaily dressed, some with bracelets and anklets all stalking hidalgo-like, and accepting salutations with a haughty lip. The hair (with the dandies of either sex) is worn turban-wise in a frizzled bush; and like the daggers of the Japanese, a pointed stock (used for a comb) is thrust gallantly among the curls. The women from this bush of hair look forth enticingly: the race cannot be compared with the Tahitian for female beauty; I doubt if the average be high; but some of the prettiest girls, and one of the handsomest women I ever saw, were Gilbertines. Butaritari, being the commercial centre of the group, is Europeanised; the coloured sacque or the white shift are common wear, the latter for the evening; the trade hat, loaded with flowers, fruit and ribbons, is unfortunately not unknown; and the characteristic female dress of the Gilberts no longer universal. The *ridi* is its name: a cutty petticoat or fringe of the smoked fibre of cocoa-nut leaf, not unlike tarry string; the lower edge not reaching the mid-thigh, the upper adjusted so low upon the haunches that it seems to cling by accident. A sneeze, you think, and the lady must surely be left destitute. 'The perilous, hairbreadth *ridi*'. . . . Yet if a pretty Gilbertiner would look her best, that must be her costume. In that, and naked otherwise, she moved with an incomparable liberty and grace and life, that marks the poetry of Micronesia. Bundle her in a gown, the charm is fled, and she wriggles like an English woman.

A tale of a tapu

On the morrow of our arrival (Sunday, 14th July 1889) our photographers were early stirring. . . . A few children followed us, mostly nude, all silent; in the clear, weedy waters of the canal some silent damsels waded, baring their brown thighs; .

Missionary and converts

. . and to one of the maniap's before the palace gate we were attracted by a low but stirring hum of speech.

The oval shed was full of men sitting cross-legged. The king was there in striped pyjamas, his rear protected by four guards with Winchesters, his air and bearing marked by unwonted spirit and decision; tumblers and black bottles went the round. . . . But the hour appeared unsuitable for a carouse; drink was besides forbidden equally by the law of the land and the canons of the church. . . . We had come, thinking to photograph him surrounded by his guard, and at the first word of the design his piety revolted. We were reminded of the day — the Sabbath — in which thou shalt take no photographs — and returned with a flea in our ear, bearing the rejected camera.

At church, a little later, I was struck to find the throne unoccupied. So nice a Sabbatarian might have found the means to be present. . . . Tom, bar-keeper at the *Sans Souci*, was in conversation with two emissaries from the court. The king, they said, wanted gin, failing which, brandy. No gin, was Tom's reply, and no brandy, but beer, if they pleased. It seems they had no use for beer, and departed sorrowing.

'Is the island on the spree?' I asked.

Such was the fact. On the 4th of July a feast had been made, and the king, at the suggestion of the whites, had raised the tapu against liquor. There is a proverb

Missionaries Maka, Marymaka, Kanoa and Mrs Kanoa

about horses; it scarce applies to the superior animal of whom it may be rather said, that any one can start him drinking, not any twenty can prevail upon him to stop. The tapu was not yet reimposed; for ten days the town had been passing the bottle or lying in hoggish sleep; and the king, moved by the Old Men and his own appetites, continued to maintain the liberty, to squander his savings on liquor, and to join in and lead the debauch. The whites were the authors of the crisis . . . in the interests of trade, they were doubtless pleased it should continue. . . .

The conduct of drunkards even at home is always matter for anxiety; and at home our populations are not armed from the highest to the lowest with revolvers and repeating rifles, neither do we go on a debauch by the whole townful —kings, magistrates, police, and army joining in one common scene of drunkenness . . . we were here in barbarous islands, rarely visited, lately and partly civilised. First and last, a really considerable number of whites have perished in the Gilberts, chiefly through their own misconduct . . . this was the chief consideration against the sudden closing of the bars; the bar-keepers stood in the immediate breach and dealt direct with madmen; too surly a refusal might at any moment precipitate a blow, and the blow might prove the signal for massacre.

Monday, 15th — At the same hour we returned to the same maniap'. Kummel (of all drinks) was served in tumblers; in the midst sat the crown prince, a fatted youth, surrounded by fresh bottles and busily plying the corkscrew; and king, chief, and commons showed the loose mouth, the uncertain joints, and the blurred and animated eye of the early drinker. It was plain we were impatiently expected; the king retired with alacrity to dress, the guards were despatched after their uniforms; as we were left to await the issue of these preparations with a shedful of tipsy natives. The orgie had proceeded further than on Sunday. The day promised to be of great heat; it was already sultry, the courtiers were already fuddled; and still the kummel continued to go round, and the crown prince to play butler . . . and a funny dog, a handsome fellow, gaily dressed, and with a full turban of frizzed hair, delighted the company with a humorous courtship of a lady in a manner not to be described. It was our diversion, in this time of waiting, to observe the gathering of the guards. They have European arms, European uniforms, and (to their sorrow) European shoes. We saw one warrior (like Mars) in the article of being armed; two men and a stalwart woman were scarce enough to boot him; and after a single appearance on parade the army is crippled for a week.

At last, the gates under the king's house opened; the army issued, one behind another, with guns and epaulettes; the colours stooped under the gateway; majesty followed in his uniform bedizened with gold lace; majesty's wife came next in a hat and feathers, and an ample trained silk gown; the royal imps succeeded; there stood the pageantry of Makin marshalled on its chosen theatre. Dickens might have told how serious they were; how tipsy; how the king melted and streamed under his cocked hat; how he took station by the larger of his two cannons — austere, majestic, but not truly vertical; how the troops huddled, and were straightened out, and clubbed again; how they and their firelocks raked at various inclinations like the masts of ships; and how an amateur photographer reviewed, arrayed, and adjusted them, to see his dispositions change before he reached the camera . . . and we had one more sight of Gilbert Island violence. In the church where we had wandered photographing, we were startled by a sudden piercing outcry. The scene, looking forth from the doors of that great hall of shadow, was unforgettable. The palms, the quaint and scattered houses, the flag of the island streaming from its tall staff, glowed with intolerable sunshine. It the midst two women rolled fighting on the grass. The combatants were the more easy to be distinguished, because the one was stripped to the *ridi* and the other wore a *holoku* of some lively colour. The first was uppermost, her teeth locked in her adversary's face, shaking her like a dog; the other impotently fought and scratched. For a moment we saw them wallow and grapple there like vermin; then the mob closed and shut them in.

It was a serious question that night if we should sleep ashore. But we were travellers, folk that had come far in quest of the adventurous; on the first sign of an adventure it would have been a singular inconsistency to have withdrawn; and we sent on board instead for our revolvers. Mindful of Taahauku, Mr Rick, Mr Osbourne and Mrs Stevenson held an assault of arms on the public highway and fired at bottles to the admiration of the natives. Captain Reid stayed on shore with us to be at hand in case of trouble, and we retired to bed at the accustomed hour, agreeably excited by the day's events. The night was exquisite, the silence enchanting; yet as I lay in my hammock looking on the strong moonshine and the quiescent palms, one ugly picture haunted me of the two women, the naked and the clad, locked in that hostile embrace. The harm done was probably not much, yet I could have looked on death and massacre with less revolt. The return to these primeval weapons, the vision of man's beastliness, of his ferality, shocked in me a deeper sense than that with which we count the cost of battles. There are elements in our state and history which it is a pleasure to forget, which it is perhaps the better wisdom not to dwell on. Crime, pestilence, and death are in the day's work; the imagination readily accepts them. It instinctively rejects, on the contrary, whatever shall call up the image of our race upon its lowest terms, as the partner of beasts, beastly itself, dwelling pell-mell and hugger-mugger, hairy man with hairy woman, in the caves of old. And yet to be just to barbarous islanders we must not forget the slums and dens of our cities: I must not forget that I have passed dinnerward through Soho, and seen that which cured me of my dinner.

Tuesday, July 16. — It rained in the night, sudden and loud, in Gilbert Island fashion. . . . Through the desert streets, and past the sleeping houses, a deputation took its way at an early hour to the palace . . . . Mrs Rick (the only white woman on the island) being a sufficient mistress of that difficult tongue, was spokeswoman; she explained to the sick monarch that I was an intimate personal friend of Queen Victoria's; that immediately on my return I should make her a report upon Butaritari; and that if my house should have been again invaded by natives, a man-of-war would be despatched to make reprisals. It was scarce the fact — rather a just and necessary parable of the fact, corrected for latitude; and it certainly told upon the king. He was much affected . . . and the missionary house was tapu'd under a fine of fifty dollars. . . . The protection gained was welcome. It had been the most annoying and not the least alarming feature of the day before, that our house was periodically filled with tipsy natives, twenty or thirty at a time, begging drink, fingering our goods, hard to be dislodged, awkward to quarrel with. Queen Victoria's friend (who was soon promoted to be her son) was free from these intrusions . . . even on our walks abroad we were guarded and prepared for; and, like great persons visiting a hospital, saw only the fair side. . . .

Hula Dancers

Wednesday, July 24. — ... Whether the Old Men recoiled from an interview with Queen Victoria's son, or whether the step flowed naturally from the fears of the king, the tapu was early that morning re-enforced; not a day too soon, from the manner the boats began to arrive thickly, and the town was filled with the big rowdy vassals of Karaiti. The effect lingered for some time on the minds of the traders; it was with the approval of all present that I helped to draw up a petition to the United States, praying for a law against the liquor trade in the Gilberts; and it was at this request that I added, under my own name, a brief testimony of what had passed — useless pains, since the whole reposes, probably unread and possibly unopened, in a pigeon-hole at Washington.

The Five Days Festival

Thursday, Juy 25. — Of all so-called dancing in the South Seas, that which I saw in Butaritari stand easily the first. The *bula*, as it may be viewed by the speedy globetrotter in Honolulu, is surely the most dull of man's inventions, and the spectator yawns under its length as at a college lecturer or a parliamentary debate. But the Gilbert Island dance leads on the mind; it thrills, rouses, subjugates; it has the essence of all art ... here is a page from my wife's diary, which proves that I was not alone in being moved. . . . 'The conductor gave the cue, and all the dancers, waving their arms, swaying their bodies, and clapping their breasts in perfect time, opened with an introductory. The performers remained seated, except two, and once three, a twice and twice a single soloist. These stood in a group making a slight movement with the feet and rhythmical quiver of the body as they sang. . . . The leading man, in an impassioned ecstasy which possessed him

143

from head to foot, seemed transfigured; once it was as though a strong wind swept over the stage — their arms, their feathered fingers thrilling with an emotion that shook my nerves as well: heads and bodies followed like a field of grain before a gust. My blood came hot and cold, tears prickled my eyes, my head whirled, I felt an almost irresistible impulse to join the dancers. . . .'

Saturday, July 27. — We had announced a performance of the magic lantern tonight in church; and this brought the king to visit us. In honour of the Black Douglas (I suppose) his usual two guardsmen were now increased to four; and the squad made an outlandish figure as they straggled after him, in straw hats, kilts and jackets. Three carried their arms reversed, the butts over their shoulders, the muzzles menacing the king's plump back; the fourth passed his weapon behind his back, and held it there with arms extended like a backboard. The visit was extraordinary long. The king, no longer galvanised with gin, said and did nothing. He sat collapsed in a chair and let a cigar go out. It was hot, it was sleepy, it was cruel dull; there was no resource but to spy in the countenance of Tebureimoa for some remainder trait of *Mr. Corpse* the butcher. His hawk nose, crudely depressed and flattened at the point, did not truly seem to us to smell of midnight murder. . . .

While the magic lantern was showing, I skulked without in the dark. The

Gilbert Islands dancers

voice of Maka (the missionary) excitedly explaining the Scripture slides, seemed to fill not the church only, but the neighbourhood . . . . a distant sound of singing arose and approached; a procession drew along the road, the hot clean smell of the men and women striking in my face delightfully. At the corner, arrested by the voice of Maka and the lightening and darkening of the church, they paused. They had no mind to go nearer, that was plain . . . staunch heathens, contemners of the missionary and his works. Of a sudden, however, a man broke from their company, took to his heels, and fled into the church; next moment three had followed him; the next it was a covey of near upon a score, all pelting for their lives. So the little band of the heathen paused irresolute at the corner, and melted before the attractions of a magic lantern, like a glacier in spring. The more staunch vainly taunted the deserters; three fled in a guilty silence, but still fled; and when at length the leader found the wit or the authority to get his troop in motion and revive the singing, it was with much diminished forces that they passed musically on up the dark road.

Meanwhile inside the luminous pictures brightened and faded. I stood for some while unobserved in the rear of the spectators when I could hear just in front of me a pair of lovers following the show with interest, the male playing the part of interpreter and (like Adam) mingling caresses with his lecture. The wild animals, a tiger in particular, and that old school-treat favourite, the sleeper and the mouse, were hailed with joy; but the chief marvel and delight was in the gospel series. Maka, in the opinion of his aggrieved wife, did not properly rise to the occasion. 'What is the matter with the man? Why can't he talk?' she cried. The matter with the man, I think, was the greatness of the opportunity; he reeled under his good fortune, and whether he did ill or well, the exposure of these pious 'phantoms' did as a matter of fact silence in all that part of the island the voice of the scoffer. 'Why then,' the word went round, 'why then, the Bible is true!' And on our return afterwards we were told the impression was yet lively, and those who had seen might be heard telling those who had not, 'O yes, it is all true; these things all happened, we have seen the pictures.' The argument is not so childish as it seems; for I doubt if these islanders are acquainted with any other mode of representation but photography; so that the picture of an event (on the old melodrama principle that 'the camera cannot lie, Joseph,') would appear strong proof of its occurrence. The fact amused us the more because our slides were some of them ludicrously silly, and one (Christ before Pilate) was received with shouts of merriment, in which even Maka was constrained to join. . . .

Sunday, July 28 (From *A Tale of Tapu*). — This day we had the afterpiece of the debauch. The king and queen, in European clothes, and followed by armed guards, attended church for the first time, and sat perched aloft in a precarious dignity under the barrel-hoops. Before the sermon His Majesty clambered from the dais, stood lopsidedly upon the gravel floor, and in a few words abjured drinking. The queen followed suit with a yet briefer allocution. All the men in church were next addressed in turn; each held up his right hand, and the affair was over — throne and church were reconciled.

Monday, July 29 (From *The Five Days' Festival*). — . . . The last stage and glory of this auspicious day was of our own providing — the second and positively the last appearance of the 'phantoms' — this was the accepted word — All round the church, groups sat outside, in the night, where they could see nothing; perhaps ashamed to enter, certainly finding some shadowy pleasure in the mere proximity. Within, about one-half of the great shed was densely packed with people. In the midst, on the royal dais, the lantern luminously smoked; . . . the pictures shone and vanished on the screen; and as each appeared there would run a hush, a whisper, a strong shuddering rustle, and a chorus of small cries among the crowd. There sat by me the mate of a wrecked schooner. 'They would think this a strange sight in Europe or the States,' said he, 'going on in a building like this, all tied with bits of string.'

Letter to Sidney Colvin
Schooner 'Equator', Apaiang lagoon, August 22nd, 1889

My dear Colvin, — . . . I am glad to say I shall be home by June next for the summer, or we shall know the reason why. For God's sake be well and jolly for the meeting. I shall be, I believe, a different character from what you have seen this long while. This cruise is up to now a huge success, being interesting, pleasant and profitable. The beachcomber is perhaps the most interesting character here; the natives are very different, on the whole, from Polynesians: they are moral, stand-offish (for good reasons), and protected by a dark tongue. It is delightful to meet the few Hawaiians (mostly missionaries) that are dotted about, with their Italian *brio* and their ready friendliness. The whites are a strange lot, many of them good, kind, pleasant fellows; others quite the lowest I have ever seen in the slums of cities. I wish I had time to narrate to you the doings and character of three white murderers (more or less proven) I have met. One, the only undoubted assassin of the lot, quite gained my affection in his big home out of a wreck, with his New Hebrides wife in her savage turban of hair and yet a perfect lady, and his three adorable little girls in Rob Roy Macgregor dresses, dancing to the hand organ, performing circus on the floor with startling effects of nudity, and curling up together on a mat to sleep, three sizes, three attitudes, three Rob Roy dresses, and six little clenched fists: the murderer meanwhile brooding and gloating over his chicks, till your whole heart went out to him; and yet his crime on the face of it was dark; disembowelling, in his own house, an old man of seventy, and him drunk. It is lunchtime, I see, and I must close with warmest love to you. I wish you were here to sit upon me when required. I will never leave the sea, I think; it is only there that a Briton lives: my poor grandfather, it is from him I inherit the taste, I fancy, and he was round many islands in his day: would you be surprised to learn that I contemplate becoming a ship-owner? I do, but it is a secret. Life is far

King Tembinok and party leaving Equator

better fun than people dream who fall asleep among the chimney stacks and telegraph wires.

Love to Henry James and others near. Ever yours, my dear fellow,
ROBERT LOUIS STEVENSON.

Husband and wife

The trader accustomed to the manners of Eastern Polynesia has a lesson to learn among the Gilberts. The *ridi* is but a spare attire; as late as thirty years back the women went naked until marriage; within ten years the custom lingered; and these facts, above all when heard in description, conveyed a very false idea of the manners of the group. A very intelligent missionary described it as a 'Paradise of naked women' for the resident whites. It was at least a platonic Paradise, where Lothario ventured at his peril. Since 1860, fourteen whites have perished on a single island, all for the same cause, all found where they had no business, and speared by some indignant father of a family; the figure was given me by one of their contemporaries who had been more prudent and survived. The strange persistence of these fourteen martyrs might seem to point to monomania or a series of romantic passions; gin is the more likely key. The poor buzzards sat alone in their houses by an open case; they drank; their brain was fired; they stumbled towards the nearest houses on chance; and the dart went through their liver. In

147

place of a Paradise the trader found an archipelago of fierce husbands and of virtuous women. 'Of course if you wish to make love to them, it's the same as anywhere else,' observed a trader innocently; but he and his companion rarely so choose.

The trader must be credited with a virtue: he often makes a kind and loyal husband. Some of the worst beachcombers in the Pacific, some of the last of the old school, have fallen in my path, and some of them were admirable to their native wives, and one made a despairing widower. . . . All these women were legitimately married. It is true that the certificate of one, when she proudly showed it, proved to run thus, that she was 'married for one night', and her gracious partner was at liberty to 'send her to hell' the next morning; but she was none the wiser or the worse for the dastardly trick.* Another, I heard, was married on a work of mine in a pirated edition; it answered the purpose as well as a Hall Bible. . . . Ten or twenty years ago it was a capital offence to raise a woman's *ridi*; to this day it is still punished with a heavy fine; and the garment itself is symbolically sacred. Suppose a piece of land to be disputed in Butaritari, the claimant who shall first hang a *ridi* on the tapu-post has gained his cause, since no one can remove or touch it but himself. The *ridi* was the badge not of the woman but the wife, the mark not of her sex but of her station. It was the collar on the slave's neck, the brand on merchandise.

Polygamy, the particular sacredness of wives, their semi-servile state, their seclusion in kings' harems, even their privilege of biting, all would seem to indicate a Mohammedan society and the opinion of the soullessness of woman. And not so in the least. It is mere appearance. After you have studied these extremes in one house, you may go to the next and find all reversed, the woman the mistress, the man only the first of her thalls. . . . There is but the one source of power and the one ground of dignity — rank. The king married a chief-woman; she became his menial and must work with her hands on Messrs. Wightmans pier. The king divorced her; she regained at once her former state and power. She married the Hawaiian sailor, and behold the man is her flunkey and can be shown the door at pleasure. Nay, and such low-born lords are even corrected physically, and, like grown but dutiful children, must endure the discipline.

We were intimate in one such household, that of Nei Takauti and Nan Tok'; I put the lady first of necessity. Nan Tok', the husband, was young, extremely handsome, of the most approved good humour, and suffering in his precarious station from suppressed high spirits. Nei Takauti, the wife, was getting old; her grown-up son by a former marriage had just hanged himself before his mother's eyes in despair at a well-merited rebuke. Perhaps she had never been beautiful, but her face was full of character, her eyes of sombre fire. She was a high chief-woman, but by a strange exception for a person of her rank, was small, spare, and

*[Theme of *The Beach of Falesa*]

sinewy, with lean small hands and corded neck. Her full dress of an evening was invariably a white chemise — and for adornment, green leaves (or sometimes white blossoms) stuck in her hair and thrust through her huge earring-holes. The husband on the contrary changed to view like a kaleidoscope. Whatever pretty thing my wife might have given to Nei Takauti — a string of beads, a ribbon, a piece of bright fabric — appeared the next evening on the person of Nan Tok'. It was plain he was a clothes-horse; that he wore livery; that, in a word, he was his wife's wife. They reversed the parts indeed, down to the last particular; it was the husband who showed himself the ministering angel in the hour of pain, while the wife displayed the apathy and heartlessness of the proverbial man.

When Nei Takauti had a headache Nan Tok' was full of attention and concern. When the husband had a cold and a racking toothache the wife heeded not, except to jeer. It was always the woman's part to fill and light the pipe; Nei Takauti handed hers in silence to the wedded page; but she carried it herself, as though the page were not entirely trusted. Thus she kept the money, but it was he who ran the errands, anxiously sedulous. A cloud on her face dimmed instantly his beaming looks; on an early visit to their maniap' my wife saw he had cause to be wary. Nan Tok' had a friend with him, a giddy young thing, of his own age and sex; and they had worked themselves into that stage of jocularity when consequences are too often disregarded. Nei Takauti mentioned her own name. Instantly Nan Tok' held up two fingers, his friend did likewise, both in an ecstasy of slyness. It was plain the lady had two names; and from the nature of their merriment and the wrath that gathered on her brow, there must be something

Nan Tok' and Nei Takauti 'at home'

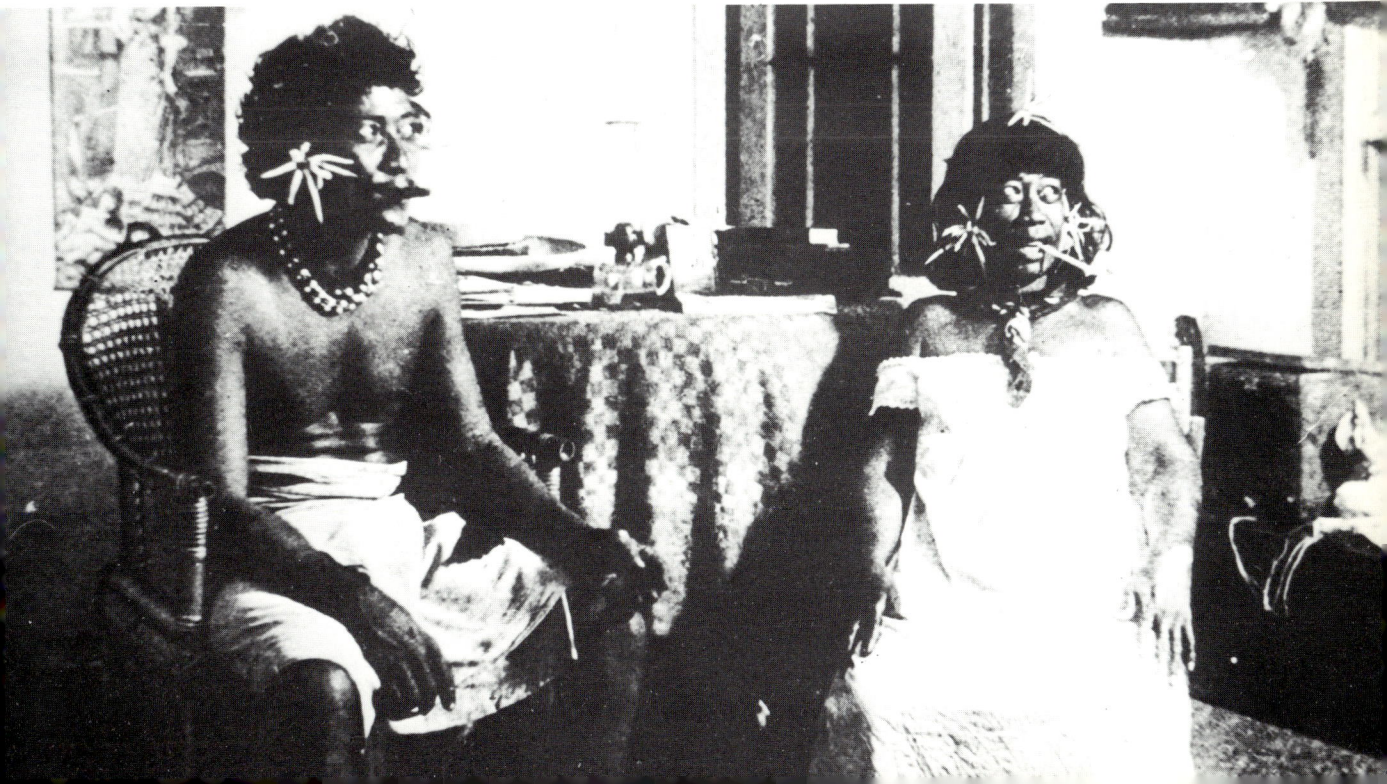

ticklish in the second. The husband pronounced it; a well-directed cocoa-nut from the hand of his wife caught him on the side of the head, and the voices and the mirth of these indiscreet young gentlemen ceased for the day.... We had once supplied them during a visit with a pipe and tobacco; and when they had smoked and were about to leave, they found themselves confronted with a problem: should they take or leave what remained of the tobacco. The piece of plug was taken up, it was laid down again, it was handed back and forth, and argued over, till the wife began to look haggard and the husband elderly. They ended by taking it, and I wager were not clear of the compound before they were sure they had decided wrong. Another time they had been given each a liberal cup of coffee, and Nan Tok' with difficulty and disaffection made an end of his. Nei Takauti had taken some, she had no mind for more, plainly conceived it would be a breach of manners to set down the cup unfinished, and ordered her wedded retainer to dispose of what was left. 'I have swallowed all I can, I cannot swallow more, it is a physical impossibility,' he seemed to say; and his stern officer reiterated her commands with secret imperative signals. Luckless dog! but in mere humanity we came to the rescue and removed the cup.

I cannot but smile over this funny household; yet I remember the good souls with affection and respect. Their attention to ourselves was surprising. The garlands are much esteemed, the blossoms must be sought far and wide; and though they had many retainers to call to their aid, we often saw themselves passing afield after the blossoms, and the wife engaged with her own hands in putting them together. It was no want of heart, only that disregard so incident to husbands, that made Nei Takauti despise the sufferings of Nan Tok'. When my wife was unwell she proved a diligent and kindly nurse; and the pair, to the extreme embarrassment of the sufferer, became fixtures in the sick-room. This rugged, capable, imperious old dame, with the wild eyes, had deep and tender qualities. Her pride in her young husband it seemed that she dissembled, fearing possibly to spoil him; and when she spoke of her dead son there came something tragic in her face. But I seemed to trace in the Gilbertines a virility of sense and sentiment which distinguishes them (like their harsh and uncouth language) from their brother islanders in the east.

The King of Apemama

There is only one great personage in the Gilberts: Tembinok' of Apemama; solely conspicuous, the hero of song, the butt of gossip. Through the rest of the group the kings are slain or fallen in tutelage: Tembinok' alone remains, the last tyrant, the last erect vestige of a dead society. The white man is everywhere else, building his houses, drinking his gin, getting in and out of trouble with the weak native governments. There is only one white on Apemama, and he on sufferance, living far from court, and hearkening and watching his conduct like a mouse in a cat's ear. Through all the other islands a stream of native visitors comes and goes, travelling by families, spending years on the grand tour. Apemama alone is left

Fanny and Louis Stevenson on bridge of Equator

upon the side, the tourist dreading to risk himself within the clutch of Tembinok'.

. . . We were scarce yet moored, however, before distant and busy figures appeared upon the beach, a boat was launched and a crew pulled out to us bringing the king's ladder. Tembinok' had once an accident; has feared ever since to intrust his person to the rotten chandlery of South Seas traders; and devised in consequence a frame of wood, which is brought on board a ship as soon as she appears, and remains lashed to her side until she leaves. . . . Not long ago he was overgrown with fat, obscured to view, and a burthen to himself. Captains visiting the island advised him to walk; and though it broke the habits of a life and the traditions of his rank, he practised the remedy with benefit. His corpulence is now portable; you would call him lusty rather than fat; but his gait is still dull, stumbling and elephantine. He neither stops nor hastens, but goes about his business with an implacable deliberation. We could never see him and not be struck with his extraordinary natural means for the theatre: a beaked profile like Dante's in the mask, a mane of long black hair, the eye brilliant, imperious and inquiring: for certain parts, and to one who could have used it, the face was a fortune. His voice matched it well, being shrill, powerful, and uncanny, with a note like a seabird's. Where there were no fashions, none to set them, few to follow them if they were set, and none to criticise, he dressed — as Sir Charles Grandison lived — 'to his own heart'. Now he wears a woman's frock, now a naval uniform; now (and more usually) figures in a masquerade costume of his own design; trousers and a singular jacket with shirt-tails, the cut and fit wonderful for island workmanship, the material always handsome, sometimes green velvet, sometimes cardinal red silk. This masquerade becomes him admirably. In the woman's frock he looks ominous and weird beyond belief. I see him now come pacing towards me in the cruel sun, solitary, a figure out of Hoffman.

A visit on board ship, such as that at which we were now assisted, makes a chief part and by far the chief diversion of the life of Tembinok'. He is not only the sole ruler, he is the sole merchant of his triple kingdom. . . . If he be pleased with his welcome and the fare he may pass days on board, and every day, and sometimes every hour, will be of profit to the ship. He oscillates between the cabin, where he is entertained with strange meats, and the trade-room, where he enjoys the pleasures of shopping on a scale to match his person. A few obsequious attendants squat by the house door, awaiting his least signal. In the boat, which has been suffered to drop astern, one or two of his wives lie covered from the sun under mats, tossed by the short sea of the lagoon, and enduring agonies of heat and tedium. This severity is now and then relaxed and the wives allowed on board. Three or four were thus favoured on the day of our arrival; substantial ladies airily attired in *ridis*. Each had a share of copra, her *peculium*, to dispose of for herself. The display in the trade-room — hats, ribbons, dresses, scents, tins of salmon — the pride of the eye and the lust of the flesh — tempted them in vain. They had but one idea — tobacco, the island currency, tantamount to minted gold; returned to shore with it, burthened but rejoicing; and late into the night, on the royal terrace, were to be seen counting the sticks by lamplight in the open air.

The king is no such economist. He is greedy of things new and foreign. House after house, chest after chest, in the palace precinct, is already crammed with clocks, musical boxes, blue spectacles, umbrellas, knitted waistcoats, bolts of stuff, tools, rifles, fowling-pieces, medicines, European foods, sewing-machines, and, what is more extraordinary, stoves: all that ever caught his eye, tickled his appetite, pleased him for its use, or puzzled him with its apparent inutility. And still his lust is unabated. He is possessed by the seven devils of the collector. He hears a thing spoken of, and a shadow comes on his face. 'I think I no got him,' he will say; and the treasures he has seem worthless in comparison. If a ship be bound for Apemama, the merchant racks his brain to hit upon some novelty. This he leaves carelessly in the main cabin or partly conceals in his own berth, so that the king shall spy it for himself. 'How much you want?' inquires Tembinok', passing and pointing. 'No, king; that too dear,' returns the trader. 'I think I like him,' says the king. This was a bowl of goldfish. On another occasion it was scented soap. 'No, king; that cost too much,' said the trader; 'too good for a Kanaka.' 'How much you got? I take him all,' replied his majesty, and became the lord of seventeen boxes at two dollars a cake. Or again, the merchant feigns the article is not for sale, is private property, an heirloom or a gift; and the trick infallibly succeeds. Thwart the king and you hold him. His autocratic nature rears at the affront of opposition. He accepts it for a challenge; sets his teeth like a hunter going at a fence; and with no mark of emotion, scarce even of interest, stolidly piles up the price. Thus, for our sins, he took a fancy to my wife's dressing-bag, a thing entirely useless to the man, and sadly battered by years of service. Early one forenoon, he came to our house, sat down, and abruptly offered to purchase it. I told him I sold nothing, and the bag at any rate was a present from a friend; but he was acquainted with these pretexts from of old, and knew what they were worth and how to meet them. He drew out a bag of English gold, sovereigns and half-sovereigns, and began to lay them one by one in silence on the table; at each fresh piece reading our faces with a look. In vain I continued to protest I was no trader; he deigned not to reply. There must have been twenty pounds on the table, he was still going on, and irritation had begun to mingle with our embarrassment, when a happy idea came to our delivery. Since his majesty thought so much of the bag, we said, we must beg him to accept it as a present. It was the most surprising turn in Tembinok's experience. He perceived too late that his persistence was unmannerly, hung his head a while in silence: then, lifting up a sheepish countenance, 'I 'shamed,' said the tyrant. It was the first and last time we heard him own to a flaw in his behaviour. Half an hour after he sent us a camphor-wood chest, worth only a few dollars — but then heaven knows what Tembinok' had paid for it. . . .

★ ★ ★ ★

The palace, or rather the ground which it includes, is several acres in extent. . . . There is no parade of guards, soldiers, or weapons; the armoury is under lock and key; and the only sentinels are certain inconspicuous old women lurking day and night before the gates. By day, these crones were often engaged in boiling syrup or the like household occupation; by night, they lay ambushed in the shadow or crouched along the palisade, filling the office of eunuchs to this harem, sole guards upon a tyrant life.

Female wardens made a fit outpost for this palace of many women. Of the number of the king's wives I have no guess; and but a loose idea of their function. He himself displayed embarrassment when they were referred to as his wives, called them himself 'my pamily' and explained they were his 'cutcheons' —cousins. We distinguished four of the crowd: the king's mother; his sister, a grave, trenchant woman, with much of her brother's intelligence; the queen proper, to whom (and to whom alone) my wife was formally presented; and the favourite of the hour, a pretty graceful girl, who sat with the king daily, and once (when he shed tears) consoled him with caresses. In the background figured a multitude of ladies, the lean, the plump, and the elephantine, some in sacque frocks, some in the hairbreadth *ridi*; high born and low, slave and mistress; from the queen to the scullion, from the favourite to the scraggy sentries at the palisade. . . . They were key-bearers, treasurers, wardens of the armoury, the napery, and the stores. Each knew and did her part to admiration. Should anything be required — a particular gun perhaps, or a particular bolt of stuff — the right queen was summoned; she came bringing the right chest, opened it in the king's presence, and displayed her charge in perfect preservation — the gun cleaned and oiled, the goods duly folded. Without delay or haste, and with the minimum of speech, the whole great establishment turned on wheels like a machine. Nowhere have I seen order more complete and pervasive. . . . Should one out of many prove faithless, should the armoury be secretly unlocked, should the crones have dozed by the palisade and the weapons find their way unseen into the village, revolution would be nearly certain, death the most probable result. Yet those whom he so trusts are all women, and all rivals.

I conceived they made rather a hero of the man. A popular master in a girls' school might, perhaps, offer a figure of his prepondering station. But then the master does not eat, sleep, live, and wash his dirty linen in the midst of his admirers; he escapes, he has a room of his own, he leads a private life; if he has nothing else, he has the holidays, and the more unhappy Tembinok' is always on the stage and on the stretch. . . .

He would come strolling over, always alone, a little before a meal-time, take a chair, and talk and eat with us like an old family friend. Gilbertine etiquette appears defective on the point of leave-taking; and there was something childish and disconcerting in Tembinok's abrupt 'I want to go home now', accompanied by a kind of ducking rise, and followed by an unadorned retreat. It was the only blot upon his manners, which were otherwise plain, decent, sensible and

Tutuila

dignified. He never stayed long nor drank much, and copied our behaviour where he perceived it to differ from his own. Very early in the day, for instance, he ceased eating with his knife. It was plain he was determined in all things to wring profit from our visit, and chiefly upon etiquette. The quality of his white visitors puzzled and concerned him; he would bring up name after name, and ask if its bearer were a 'big chiep', or even a 'chiep' at all. His vocabulary is apt and ample to an extraordinary degree. God knows where he collected it, but by some instinct or some accident he has avoided all profane or gross expressions. . . . It was my part not only to supply new information, but to correct the old. We were showing the magic lantern; a slide of Windsor Castle was put in, the 'outch (house)'of Victoreea. 'How many pathom (fathom) he high?' he asked, and I was dumb before him. It was the builder, the indefatigable architect of palaces, that spoke; collector though he was, he did not collect useless information; and all his questions had a purpose. . . . 'My patha (father) he tell me', or 'White man he tell me', would be his constant beginning. 'You think he lie?' Sometimes I thought he did. A schooner captain had told him of Captain Cook; the king was much interested in the story; and turned for more information — not to Mr Stephen's Dictionary, nor to the *Britannica*, but to the Bible in the Gilbert Island version (which consists chiefly of the New Testament and the Psalms). Here he sought long and earnestly; Paul he found, and Festus, and Alexander the coppersmith: no word of Cook. The inference was obvious: the explorer was a myth. So hard it is,

155

even for a man of great natural parts like Tembinok', to grasp the ideas of a new society and culture. . . .

As the time approached for our departure Tembinok' became greatly changed; a softer, a more melancholy, and in particular, a more confidential man appeared in his stead. . . . We showed fireworks one evening on the terrace. It was a heavy business; the sense of separation was in all our minds and the talk languished. The king was specially affected, sat disconsolate on his mat, and often sighed. Presently after we said goodnight and withdrew Tembinok' detained Mr Osbourne, patting the mat beside him saying: 'Sit down. I feel bad, I like talk . . . I very sorry you go. Miss Stlevens (Fanny), he good man, woman he good man, boy he good man; all good man. Woman he smart all the same man. My woman' (glancing towards his wives) 'he good man, no very smart. I think Miss Stlevens he big chief all the same cap'n man-o-wa'. I think Miss Stlevens he rich all the same me. All go schoona. I very sorry. My father he go, my uncle he go, my cousins, he go, Miss Stlevens he go: all go. You no see king cry before. King all the same man: feel bad, he cry. I very sorry.' . . .

In the morning it was the common topic in the village that the king had wept. To me he said: 'Last night I no can 'peak: too much here,' laying his hand upon his bosom. 'Now you go away all the same my family. My brothers, my uncle go away. All the same.'

Letter to Sidney Colvin
Equator Town, Apemama, October 1889

. . . The king is a great character — a thorough tyrant, very much of a gentleman, a poet, a musician, a historian, or perhaps rather more of a genealogist — it is strange to see him lying in his house among a lot of his wives (nominal wives) writing the History of Apemama in an account-book; his description of one of his own songs, which he sang to me himself, as 'about sweethearts, and trees, and the sea — and no true all-the-same lie', seems about as compendious a definition of lyric poetry as a man could ask. Tembinok' is here the great attraction: all the rest is heat and tedium and villainous dazzle, and yet more villainous mosquitoes. We are like to be here, however, many a long week before we get away, and then whither? A strange trade this voyaging: so vague, so bound-down, so helpless. Fanny has been planting some vegetables, and we have actually onions and radishes coming up: ah, onion-despiser, were you but a while in a low island, how your heart would leap at sight of a coster's barrow! I think I could shed tears over a dish of turnips. No doubt we shall all be glad to say farewell to low islands — I had near said forever. They are very tame; and I begin to read up the directory and pine for an island with a profile, a running brook, or were it only a well among the rocks. The thought of a mango came to me early this morning and set my greed on edge; but you would not know what a mango is, so —

I have been thinking a great deal of you and the Monument of late, and even tried to get my thoughts into a poem, hitherto without success. God knows how you are: I begin to weary dreadfully to see you — well, in nine months, I hope; but that seems a long time. I wonder what has befallen me too, that flimsy part of me that lives (or dwindles) in the public mind; and what has befallen *The Master*, and what kind of a Box the Merry Box has been found. It is odd to know nothing of all this. We had an old woman to do devil-work for you about a month ago, in a Chinaman's house on Apaiang (August 23rd or 24th). You should have seen the crone with a noble masculine face, like that of an old crone [sic], a body like a man's (naked all but the feathery female girdle), knotting cocoanut leaves and muttering spells: Fanny and I, and the good captain of the *Equator*, and the Chinaman and his native wife and sister-in-law, all squatting on the floor about the sibyl; and a crowd of dark faces watching from behind her shoulder (she sat right in the doorway) and tittering aloud with strange, appalled, embarrassed laughter at each fresh adjuration. She informed us you were in England, not travelling and now no longer sick; she promised us a fair wind next day, and we had it, so I cherish the hope she was as right about Sidney Colvin. The ship-owning has rather petered out since I last wrote, and a good many other plans beside.

Health? Fanny very so-so; I pretty right upon the whole, and getting through plenty work: I know not quite how, but it seems to me not bad and in places funny . . . a hot-bed of strange characters and incidents: Lord, how different from Europe and the Pallid States! Farewell. Heaven knows when this will get to you. I burn to be in Sydney and have news.

R.L.S.

Letter to Mrs Margaret Stevenson
Schooner Equator, *at sea 240 miles from Samoa*
Sunday, December 1st, 1889

My dear Mother, — We are drawing (we fondly hope) to the close of another voyage like that from Tahiti to Hawaii; we sailed from Butaritari on the 4th November, and since then have lain becalmed under cataracts of rain, or kicked about in purposeless squalls. We were sixteen souls in this small schooner, eleven in the cabin; our confinement and overcrowding in the wet weather was excessive; we lost our foretopmast in a squall; the sails were continually being patched (we had but the one suit) and with all attention we lost the jigtopsail almost entirely and the staysail and mainsail are far through. To complete the discomfort, we have carried a very mild weatherglass. . . . I wonder are you already so far out of key with the South Seas, that 79 degrees at noon will seem warm to you? You should have seen the great coats out! I myself wore two wool undershirts, a knitted waistcoat — the gift of the King of Apemama — and a flannel blazer; and I was seriously thinking of a flannel shirt, when the cold let up. My birthday was a great event; Mr Rich, the agent of the firm at Butaritari, who make on this trip one of the eleven being in the cabin, had his on the twelfth; so we had two days' festivity — champagne, music, the capture of sharks, dolphins and skipjack — mighty welcome additions to our table. . . .

We had a fine alert once; a reef ahead — three positions indicated, our own disputed — a very heavy sea running — the boats cleared and supplied with bread and water, our little packets made (medicines, papers and woollen clothes) and the poor passenger for Waikiki trying rather ruefully to insure his little all which was on board. It was rather fine going to bed that night; though had we struck the reef the boat voyage of four or five hundred miles would have been no joke.

Fanny has stood the hardships of this rough cruise wonderfully; but I do not think I could enforce her to another of the same. I've been first rate, though I am now done for lack of green food. Joe [Strong] is, I fear, really ill; and Lloyd has bad sores in his leg. We shall send Joe on to Sydney by the first steamer; and Lloyd, Fanny and I shall stay on awhile (time quite vague) in Samoa. Write to Sydney. We shall turn up in England by May or June. Ever your afft. son.

R.L.S.

Letter to Sidney Colvin
Schooner Equator, at sea 190 miles off Samoa
Monday, December 2, 1889

My dear Colvin, — We are just nearing the end of our long cruise. Rain, calms, squalls, bang — there's the foreto mast gone; rain, calm, squalls, away with the stay-sail; more rain, more calm, more squalls; a prodigious heavy sea all the time, and the *Equator* staggering and hovering like a swallow in a storm; and the cabin, a great square, crowded with wet human beings, and the rain avalanching the deck, and the leaks dripping everywhere: Fanny in the midst of fifteen males, bearing up wonderfully. But such voyages are at the best a trial.

. . . I am minded not to stay very long in Samoa and confine my studies there (as far as anyone can forecast) to the history of the late war. My book is now practically modelled: if I can execute what is designed, there are few better books now extant on this globe, bar the epics, and the big tragedies, and histories, and the choice lyric poetics and a novel or so — none. But it is not executed yet; and let not him that putteth on his armour, vaunt himself. At least, nobody has had such stuff, such wild stories, such beautiful scenes, such singular intimacies, such manners and traditions, so incredible a mixture of the beautiful and horrible, the savage and civilised. I will give you some idea of the table of contents, which ought to make your mouth water. I propose to call the book *The South Seas*; it is rather a large title, but not many people have seen more of them than I, perhaps no one — certainly no one capable of using the material. . . .

Even so sketched it makes sixty chapters, not less than 300 Cornhill pages; and

I suspect not much under 500. Samoa has yet to be accounted for: I think it will be all history, and I shall work in observations on Samoan manners, under the similar heads in other Polynesian islands. It is possible, though unlikely, that I may add a passing visit to Fiji or Tonga, or even both; but I am growing impatient to see yourself, and I do not want to be later than June of coming to England. Anyway, you see it will be a large work, and as it will be copiously illustrated, the Lord knows what it will cost. We shall return, God willing, by Sydney, Ceylon, Suez, and, I guess, Marseilles the many-masted (copyright epithet). I shall likely pause a day or two in Paris, but all that is too far ahead — although now it begins to look near — so near, and I can hear the rattle of the hansom up Endell Street and see the gates swing back, and feel myself jump out upon the Monument steps — Hosanna! — home again. My dear fellow, now that my father is done with his troubles, and 17 Heriot Row no more than a mere shell, you and that gaunt old Monument in Bloomsbury are all that I have in view when I use the word home; some passing thoughts there may be of the rooms at Skerryvore, and the black-birds in the chine on a May morning; but the essence is S.C. and the Museum. Suppose, by some damned accident, you were no more; well, I should return just the same, because of my mother and Lloyd, whom I now think to send to Cambridge; but all the spring would have gone out of me, and ninety per cent. of the attraction lost. I will copy for you here a copy of verses made in Apemama.

> I heard the pulse of the besieging sea
> Throb far away all night. I heard the wind
> Fly crying, and convulse tumultuous palms.
> I rose and strolled. The isle was all bright sand,
> And flailing fans and shadows of the palms:
> The heaven all moon, and wind, and the blind vault —
> The keenest planet slain, for Venus slept.
> The King, my neighbour, with his host of wives,
> Slept in the precinct of the palisade:
> Where single, in the wind, under the moon,
> Among the slumbering cabins, blazed a fire,
> Sole street-lamp and the only sentinel.
>   To other lands and nights my fancy turned,
> To London first, and chiefly to your house,
> The many-pillared and the well-beloved.
> There yearning fancy lighted; there again
> In the upper room I lay and heard far off
> The unsleeping city murmur like a shell;
> The muffled tramp of the Museum guard
> Once more went by me; I beheld again
> Lamps vainly brighten the dispeopled street;

View of Apia harbour, Samoa

Again I longed for the returning morn,
The awaking traffic, the bestirring birds,
The consentaneous trill of tiny song
That weaves round monumental cornices
A passion charm of beauty: most of all,
For your right foot I wearied, and your knock
That was the glad reveille of my day.
     Lo, now, when to your task in the great house
At morning through the portico you pass,
One moment glance where, by the pillared wall,
Far-voyaging island gods, begrimed with smoke,
Sit now unworshipped, the rude monument
Of faiths forgot and races undivined;
Sit now disconsolate, remembering well
The priest, the victim, and the songful crowd,
The blaze of the blue noon, and that huge voice
Incessant, of the breakers on the shore.
As far as these from their ancestral shrine,
So far, so foreign, your divided friends
Wander, estranged in body, not in mind.

Letter to Charles Baxter
Samoa, December 1889

My dear Baxter, — . . . I cannot return until I have seen either Tonga or Fiji or both: and I must not leave here till I have finished my collections on the war — a very interesting bit of history, the truth often very hard to come at, and the search (for me) much complicated by the German tongue, from the use of which I have desisted (I suppose) these fifteen years. The last two days I have been mugging with a dictionary from five to six hours a day; besides this, I have to call upon, keep sweet, and judiciously interview all sorts of persons — English, American, German and Samoan. It makes a hard life; above all, as after every interview I have to come and get my notes straight on the nail. . . .

Samoa, Apia at least, is far less beautiful than the Marquesas or Tahiti: a more gentle scene, gentler acclivities, a tamer face of nature; and this much aided for the wanderer, by the great German plantations with their countless regular avenues of palms. The island has beautiful rivers, with pleasant pools and waterfalls and overhanging verdure, and often a great volume of sound, so that once I thought I was passing near a mill, and it was only the voice of the river. I am not specially attracted by the people; but they are courteous; the women very attractive, and dress lovely; the men purposeful, well set up, tall, lean and dignified. . . .

R. L. STEVENSON

PART THREE

THIRD VOYAGE
April to September 1890

In the trading steamer *Janet Nicoll*, which set out from Sydney and followed a very devious course, extending as far as Penrhyn in the Eastern to the Marshall Islands in the Western Pacific.

R.L.S.

Letter to Charles Baxter
Februar den zen 1890
Dampfer Lubeck zwischen Apia und Sydney

My dear Charles, — I have got one delightful letter from you, and heard from my mother of your kindness in going to see her. Thank you for that: you can in no way more touch and serve me. . . . Ay, ay, it is sad to sell 17 [Heriot Row]; sad and fine were the old days: when I was away in Apemama, I wrote two copies of verse about Edinburgh and the past, so ink black, so golden bright. I will send them, if I can find them for they will say something to you, and indeed one is more than half addressed to you. This is it —

TO MY OLD COMRADES

Do you remember — can we e'er forget?
How, in the coiled perplexities of youth,
In our wild climate, in our scowling town,
We gloomed and shivered, sorrowed, sobbed, and feared?
The belching winter wind, the missile rain,
The rare and welcome silence of the snows,
The laggard morn, the haggard day, the night,
The grimy spell of the nocturnal town,
Do you remember? — Ah, could one forget!
As when the fevered sick that all night long
Listed the wind intone, and hear at last
The ever-welcome voice of the chanticleer
Sing in the bitter hour before the dawn —
With sudden ardour, these desire the day:
        (Here a squall sends all flying.)
So sang in the gloom of youth the bird of hope;
So we, exulting, hearkened and desired.
For lo! in the palace porch of life
We huddled with chimeras from within —
How sweet to hear! — the music swelled and fell
And through the breach of the revolving doors
What dreams of splendour blinded us and fled!
I have since then contended and rejoiced;
Amid the glories of the house of life
Profoundly entered, and the shrine beheld;
Yet when the lamp from my expiring eyes
Shall dwindle and recede, the voice of love
Fall insignificant on my closing ears,
What sound shall come but the old cry of the wind

In our inclement city? what returns
But the image of the emptiness of youth,
Filled with the sound of footsteps and that voice
Of discontent and rapture and despair?
So, as in darkness, from the magic lamp,
The momentary pictures gleam and fade
And perish, and the night resurges — these
Shall I remember, and then all forget.

They're pretty second-rate, but felt. I can't be bothered to copy the other.

I have bought 314½ acres of beautiful land in the bush behind Apia; when we get the house built, the garden laid, and cattle in the place, it will be something to fall back on for shelter and food; and if the island could stumble into political quiet, it is conceivable it might even bring a little income. . . . We range from 600 to 1500 feet, have five streams, waterfalls, precipices, profound ravines, rich tablelands, fifty head of cattle on the ground (if anyone could catch them), a great view of forest, sea, mountains, the warships in the haven: really a noble place. Some day you are to take a long holiday and come and see it; it has been all planned.

With all these irons in the fire, and cloudy prospects, you may be sure I was pleased to hear a good account of business. I believed *The Master* was a sure card: I wonder why Henley thinks it grimy; grim it is, God knows, but sure not grimy, else I am the more deceived. I am sorry he did not care for it; I place it on the line with *Kidnapped* myself. We'll see as time goes on whether it goes above or falls below.

R.L.S.

*Vailima Papers: Excerpt from An Open Letter
to the Reverend Dr Hyde of Honolulu*

[in defence of Father Damien who ministered to the lepers of Molokai until he died of the disease in 1889]

Sydney, February 25, 1890

. . . Damien is dead and already somewhat ungratefully remembered in the field of his labours and sufferings. 'He was a good man, but very officious,' says one. Another tells me he had fallen (as other priests so easily do) into something of the ways and habits of thought of a Kanaka; but he had the wit to recognise the fact, and the good sense to laugh at it. A plain man it seems he was; I cannot find he was a popular. . . .

Of Damien I begin to have an idea. He seems to have been a man of the peasant class, certainly of the peasant type; shrewd, ignorant and bigoted, yet with an open mind, and capable of receiving and digesting a reproof if it were bluntly

Auckland harbour

administered; superbly generous in the least thing as well as in the greatest, and as ready to give his last shirt (although not without human grumbling) as he had been to sacrifice his life; essentially indiscreet and officious, which made him a troublesome colleague; domineering in all his ways, which made him incurably unpopular with the Kanakas, but yet destitute of real authority, so that his boys laughed at him and he must carry out his wishes by the means of bribes. He learned to have a mania for doctoring; and set up the Kanakas against the remedies of his regular rivals: perhaps if anything matter at all in the treatment of such a disease? the worst thing that he did, and certainly the easiest.

The best and worst of the man appear very plainly in his dealings with Mr Chapman's money; he had originally laid it out entirely for the benefit of Catholics, and even so not wisely; but after a long, plain talk, he admitted his error fully and revised the list. The sad state of the boys' home is in part the result of his lack of control; in part, of his own slovenly ways and false ideas of hygiene. Brother officials used to call it 'Damien's Chinatown'. 'Well,' they would say, 'your Chinatown keeps growing.' And he would laugh with perfect good nature, and adhere to his errors with perfect obstinacy. So much I have gathered of truth about this plain, noble human brother and father of ours; his imperfections are the traits of his face, by which we know him for our fellow; his martyrdom and his example nothing can lessen or annul; and only a person here on the spot can properly appreciate their greatness.

Letter to Mrs Margaret Stevenson
Union Club, Sydney, March 5, 1890

My dear Mother, — I understand the family keeps you somewhat informed. For myself I am in such a whirl of work and society, I can ill spare a moment. My health is excellent and has been here tried by abominable wet weather, and (what's waur?) dinners and lunches. As this is likely to be our metropolis, I have tried to lay myself out to be sociable with an eye to yoursel'. Several niceish people have turned up: Fanny has an evening, but she is about at the end of the virtuous effort, and shrinks from the approach of any fellow creature.

Have you seen Hyde's (Dr not Mr) letter about Damien? This has been one of my concerns; I have an answer in the press ... to come out as a pamphlet; of which I make of course a present to the publisher. I am not a cannibal, I would not eat the flesh of Dr Hyde — and it is conceivable it will make a noise in Honolulu. I have struck as hard as I knew how; nor do I think my answer can fail to do away (in the minds of all who see it) with the effect of Hyde's incredible and really villainous production. What a mercy I wasn't this man's *guest* in the *Morning Star*! I think it would have broke my heart.

Time for me to go! I remain, with love,

R.L.S.

Letter to Charles Baxter
Union Club, Sydney, March 7th, 1890

My dear Charles, — I did not send off the enclosed before from laziness; having gone quite sick, and being a blooming prisoner here in the club, and indeed in my bedroom. I was in receipt of your letters and your ornamental photo, and was delighted to see how well you looked, and how reasonably well I stood. ... I am sure I shall never come back home except to die; I may do it, but shall always think of the move as suicidal, unless a great change comes over me, of which as yet I see no symptom. This visit to Sydney has smashed me handsomely; and yet I made myself a prisoner here in the club upon my first arrival. This is not encouraging for further ventures; Sydney winter — or, I might almost say, Sydney spring, for I came when the worst was over — is so small an affair, comparable to our June depression at home in Scotland. ... The pipe is right again; it was the springs that had rusted, and ought to have been oiled. Its voice is now that of an angel; but,

Lord! here in the club I dare not wake it! Conceive my impatience to be in my own backwoods and raise the sound of minstrelsy. What pleasures are to be compared with those of the Unvirtuous Vituoso. Yours ever affectionately, the Unvirtuous Virtuoso,

ROBERT LOUIS STEVENSON

Letter to Sidney Colvin
S.S. Janet Nicoll, *off Upolu, Spring 1890*

My dearest Colvin, — I was sharply ill at Sydney, cut off, right out of bed, in this steamer on a fresh island cruise, and have already reaped the benefit. . . . The truth is, I fear, this life is the only one that suits me; so long as I cruise in the South Seas, I shall be well and happy — alas, no, I do not mean that, and *absit omen!* — I mean that, so soon as I cease from cruising, the nerves are strained, the decline commences, and I steer slowly but surely back to bedward. We left Sydney, had a cruel, rough passage to Auckland, for the *Janet* is the worst roller I was ever aboard

Oxford Hotel, Sydney

Sydney Harbour

of. I was confined to my cabin, ports closed, self shied out of the berth, stomach (pampered till the day I left on a diet of perpetual egg-nog) revolted at ship's food and ship eating, in a frowsy bunk, clinging with one hand to the plate, with the other to the glass, and using the knife and fork (except at intervals) with the eyelid. No matter: I picked up hand over hand. After a day in Auckland, we set sail again; were blown up in the main cabin with calcium fires as we left the bay. Let no man say I am unscientific: when I ran, on the alert, out of my stateroom, and found the main cabin incarnadined with the glow of the last scene of a pantomime, I stopped dead: 'What is this?' said I. 'This ship is on fire, I see that; but why a pantomime?' And I stood and reasoned the point, until my head was so muddled with the fumes that I could not find the companion. A few seconds later, the captain had to enter crawling on his belly, and took days to recover (if he has recovered) from the fumes. By singular good fortune, we got the hose down in time and saved the ship, but Lloyd lost most of his clothes and a great part of our photographs was destroyed! Fanny saw the native sailors tossing overboard a blazing trunk; she stopped them in time, and behold it contained my manuscripts. Thereafter we had three (or two) days fine weather: then got into a gale of wind, with rain and a vexatious sea. As we drew into our anchorage a man ashore told me afterwards the sight of the *Janet Nicoll* made him sick; and indeed it was rough play, though nothing to the night before. All through this gale I worked four to six hours per diem, spearing the ink-bottle like a flying fish, and holding my papers together as I might. For, of all things, what I was at was history — the Samoan business — and I had to turn from one to another of these piles of manuscript notes, and from one page to another in each. . . . All the same, this history is a godsend for a voyage; I can put in time, getting events co-ordinated and the narrative distributed, when my much-heaving numskull would be incapable of finish or fine style. . . . We met the missionary barque *John Williams*. I tell you it was a great day for Savage Island; the path up the cliffs was crowded with gay islandresses (I like that feminine plural) who wrapped me in their embraces, and picked my pockets of all my tobacco, with a manner which a touch

Map of Cruise of Janet Nicoll

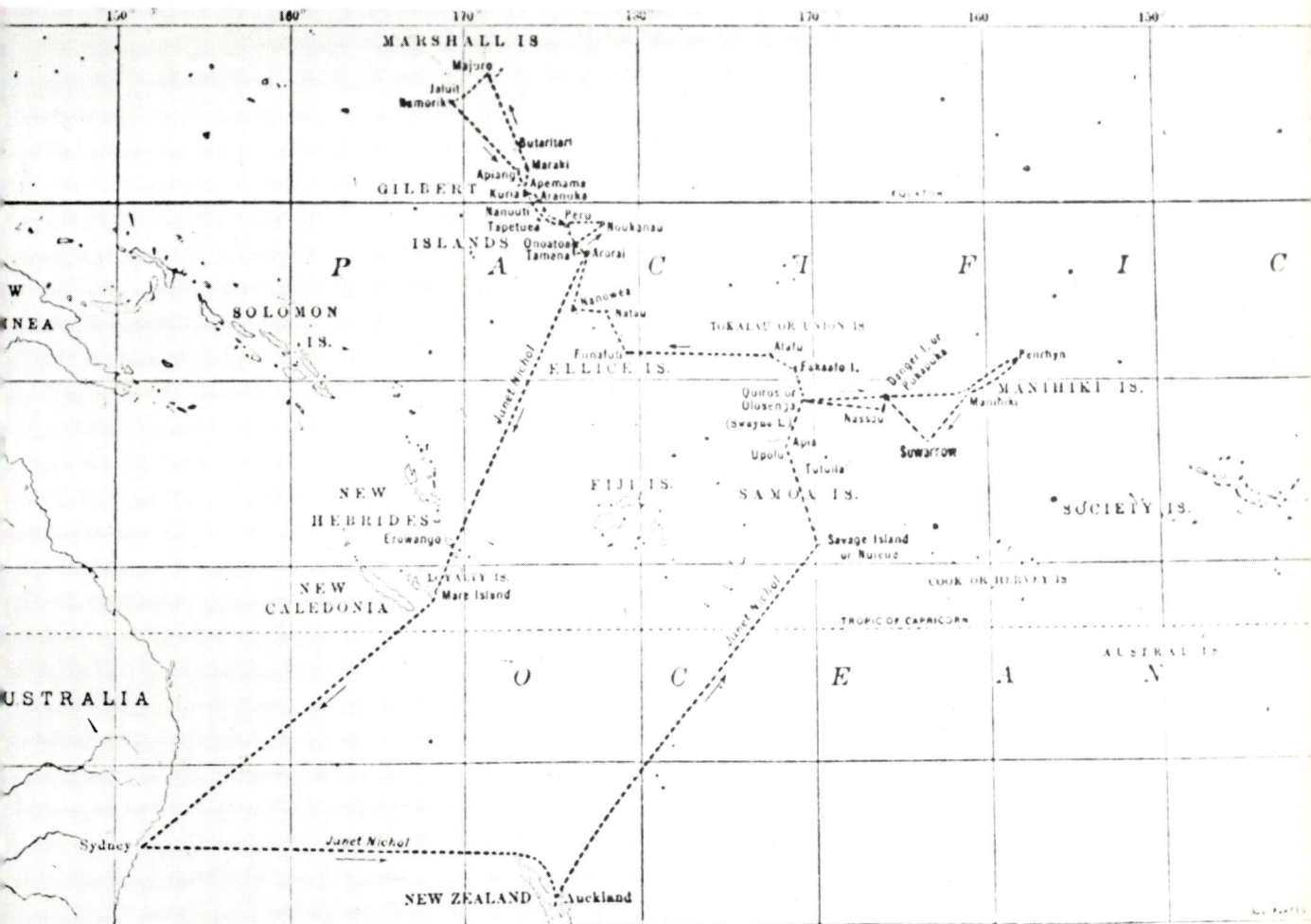

would have made revolting, but as it was, was simply charming, like the Golden Age. One pretty, little, stalwart minx, with a red flower behind her ear, had searched me with extraordinary zeal; and when, soon after, I missed my matches, I accused her (she still following us) of being the thief. After some delay, and with a subtle smile, she produced the box, gave me *one match*, and put the rest away again. Too tired to add more. Your most affectionate

R.L.S.

From the cruise of the Janet Nicoll *among the South Sea Islands*
(a diary by Mrs Robert Louis Stevenson, 1890)
[Off Friendly Is.]

18th April. — . . . Coloured fire and thick white vapour belching from our ports must have given us a very strange and alarming aspect. Lloyd looked over the opposite side of our ship and saw the ports there, also, vomiting vapour like a factory. To our surprise the cartridge-boxes were only slightly scorched. Our personal loss, however, has been very severe. About ninety photographs were destroyed and all of Lloyd's clothes except those on his back. Neither he nor I have even a toothbrush left. The annoying thing is that Tin Jack [a fellow passenger] lost nothing whatever. Lloyd is very bitter about the discrimination shown in the matter of trousers by the fire. I stopped a couple of black boys just in time to prevent them throwing overboard a blazing valise containing four large boxes of Louis's papers. A black bag, its contents at present unknown, is burned, and innumerable small necessaries that conduce to comfort on shipboard are lost. I have ever since been in a tremor lest Louis have a haemorrhage. If he does, I shall feel inclined to do something very desperate to the chemist, who, for the sake of a few shillings, put us all in such deadly peril. A horrid smell still hangs about the place and everyone feels ill. Though I hardly breathed in the room, I have a heavy oppression on my chest, and my throat and lungs burn as though I were inhaling pepper. From the time we left Auckland, the water as been as smooth as glass, and there has been no jarring or knocking about; the stuff must have gone off by a simple spontaneous combustion.

21st April. — Still drying the remains of Lloyd's clothes, burned and wet in the fire and discovering more and more losses. . . . Both our cameras escaped as by magic.

26th April. — The desire to own an island is still burning in my breast. In this neighbourhood, nearer Samoa, is just the island I want, owned, unfortunately, by a man in Tahiti. It is called Nassau and is said to be uninhabited.

Last night an immense rat ran over me in bed, and Mr Henderson had the same unpleasant experience. In the hold of the *Janet* are a number of pure white rats with red eyes, which appeared of themselves quite mysteriously. The captain will not allow them to be harmed, which I think is very nice and sentimental of

'A pretty, little, stalwart minx'

Marshall island canoe

him. It was amusing to see our dog's perplexity when we came to anchor, and put his head out of a porthole to have a look at Auckland. His tail expressed alarmed surprise. . . .

Mr Henderson has just told us as a secret that our next island will be Upolu, Samoa, and we are now as wildly excited as the second steward (who took his 'billet' under the head steward from a romantic hope of seeing Samoa, of which he had once read a description in a newspaper). On Wednesday afternoon, at four o'clock, we shall arrive at Apia, and the next morning, at break of day, off we fly to Vailima. As we were discussing the subject, the captain called out that there was a white rat in his cabin and he wished to catch and tame it, so I ran to help him. It was under his bed, he said, and the loveliest rat in the world. As he was dilating on its beauty, out it flashed, jumping on him and rebounding against my breast like a fluff of white cotton wool. The captain laughed and screamed with shrill, hysterical cries, in which I joined, while the loveliest rat in the world scurried away.

27th April. — The weather really abominable, so cold that I have had to put on a flannel bodice. . . . After I had closed my diary last night Mr Henderson got out the chart and showed us his own islands and the supposed location of Victoria Island which he is looking for. I offered to toss him for the latter, to which he agreed. Louis threw up a piece of money and I won. I have yet, however, to find Victoria.

Nuieue has not yet recovered from the effects of last year's hurricane, and we shall not get many delicacies here. There are no ripe cocoanuts, few bananas, and no breadfruit. Someone said that I could get spring onions. 'How do they grow them?' I asked; meaning did they sow seeds or plant sets. 'On the graves,' was the rather startling answer.

Last night Mr Henderson pulled off a rat's tail. He thought to pull the rat from a hole from which the tail protruded, but the tail came off, and the rat ran away. The captain tells me that there is generally a plague of flies in Nuieue. It is too cold for them now, but usually when the natives come out in their canoes, their backs especially, are black with flies. Someone has sent me a basket of bananas almost too sweet and rich, also some excellent oranges. I have mended the bellows of our camera, where it has been eaten by cockroaches, with sticking-plaster.

28th. — Steamed round to the other side of the island to the missionary station . . . we watched the *John Williams* (the missionary ship on her way to Samoa) plunging to and fro, now close under the cliffs, now skirting the *Janet*, now fetching our hearts in our mouths as she stayed, and forereached in staying, till you would have thought she had leaves on her jib-boom. We actually got up the camera to take a photograph of the expected shipwreck. We were told afterward that it was only Captain Turpie showing off his seamanship. . . .

Mr Henderson and Louis came back with some return labour boys for Danger Island. One who had signed to serve for five years had been waiting another three for a vessel to take him home. He was once disappointed, and nearly died of it. I am thankful he had this opportunity. (The 'labour boys' do, sometimes, die of homesickness. A black boy called Arriki whom we hired did so die after we left Samoa. The man to whom he was assigned by the German firm told me that both Arriki and a friend of his began to droop and become sullen, and then went quite mad; soon after they died at about the same time from no apparent disease, but he said he knew the symptoms — 'just plain homesickness for a cannibal island'. Arriki, in a moment of confidence, once described to me his life in his own land. It seemed to consist of flight from one unsafe spot to another, with death hunting on every hand. Both his father and mother had been killed and eaten, with the most of his friends; and yet Arriki died of homesickness.)

4th May. — Ran through a light squall in the night and sighted Danger Island at four in the morning. . . . We could see the natives gathering on the beach in great force. They seemed thunderstruck at the sight of a vessel with furled sails moving so rapidly against a strong headwind, the *Janet* being the first steamer that had touched at Pukapuka. As soon as our passengers were recognised, a joyful shout ran up and down the beach, and canoes were launched and paddled out to meet us. When they were just abreast of us Captain Henry blew the steam-whistle. The natives were appalled; every paddle stopped short, and the crowds on the beach seemed stricken to stone . . . it was some time before they took heart and resumed their paddling. The king, a shabbily clad man of rather mean appearance, was among them.

The meeting between the long-parted friends was very pretty and touching. I like their mode of showing affection better than ours. They took hands and pressed their faces together lightly with a delicate sniff, as I have often seen a white mother caress her baby. . . . The sheep, which the strangers saw for the first time, were studied with much interest. A group of middle-aged respectable men stood off at some distance and whistled to the sheep as though they were dogs; getting no response, they ventured a little nearer, when one of the sheep happened to move. The crowd fell back in dire confusion, and one man who had been in the van, but now occupied a rear position, asked in a trembling voice if the bite of those animals was very dangerous. . . . When a ship comes in, the natives, men, women and children, often smoke the strong trade tobacco until they fall down insensible, sometimes becoming convulsed as in epilepsy.

The trader, a half-caste, had already boarded the *Janet* in a boat of his own, but his wife, a stout, good-natured, sensible-looking woman, was waiting on the beach to receive us. She at once took possession of me as her right, and I was triumphantly swept off to her house, the crowd at our heels; here we were regaled on cocoanuts, while all the population who could crowd into the room gazed on us unwinking. The windows, also, were filled, which cut off the air and made the place rather suffocating. The children were made to sit down in the front row so that the older people could see over their heads. One old woman made me feel quite uncomfortable. Her eyes remained fixed, her jaw dropped, and nothing for a single moment diverted her attention from what she evidently regarded as a shocking and wonderful spectacle. Natives have said that the first sight of white people is dreadful, as they look like corpses walking. I have myself been startled by the sight of a crowd of whites after having seen only brown-skinned people for a long time. Louis has a theory that we whites were originally albinos. Certainly we are not a nice colour. I remember as a child the words 'flesh colour' were sickening to me, and I could not bear to see them in my paint-box. . . .

. . . Mr Hird recalls the following grisly incident that occurred when he was stopping on Penrhyn. A man who was paralysed on one side had a convulsion which caused spasmodic contractions on the other side. One of the sick man's family began at once to make a coffin. 'But the man's not dead,' said Mr Hird. 'Oh yes,' was the reply; 'he's dead enough; it's the third time he has done this, so we are going to bury him.' Mr Hird went to the native missionary, but his remonstrances had no effect; he kept on protesting until the last moment. 'Why look,' he said, 'the man's limbs are quivering.' 'Oh that's only live flesh,' was the reply, and someone fell to pommelling the poor wretch to quiet the 'live flesh'. The belief was that the man's spirit had departed long before and a devil who wished to use the body for his own convenience had been keeping the flesh alive. Mr Hird thinks that the man was insensible when buried and must soon have died.

At another time some natives had been 'waking' a corpse; tired out, they all fell asleep except a single man who acted as 'watcher'. By and by he, too, dropped off. The party were awakened by a great noise. The watcher explained that he had been napping and suddenly opened his eyes to behold the dead man sitting up. 'A corpse sitting up just like this!' he exclaimed indignantly; 'but I was equal to him; I ran at him and knocked him down, and now he's decently quiet again.' And so he was, dead as a door-nail from the blow he had received.

7th June. — Have been lying at Nanomea, the last of the Ellices we shall visit, for three days, unable to get the cargo on board till today owing to the fearful surf. A good many canoes are broken to pieces, and our own boats have had many escapes. . . . It is always a great pleasure to the natives to help raise the ship's boats to the davits for the night. They know that white sailors make a sort of cry or 'chanty' when hauling on a rope, so they, too, try to do the correct thing. The result is a noise very like a mob of schoolgirls letting loose a confusion of soprano screams. No one would suspect the sounds to come from the throats of men. Our own black sailors are the same; we hear them screaming and laughing in the forecastle exactly like girls. We are so used to island life that it has but just struck us as odd and picturesque that our almost naked sailors (they wear only a short *lava-lava* round their loins) should be working in wreaths like queens of the May.

It is only today that any women have been able to get on board. . . . They began pulling off their rings to put on my hands; I did not like taking their rings, but I need have had no scruples, for one of them with prompt energy removed a gold ring from my finger to her own. These exchanges made, they fell to examining my clothes, which filled them with admiration. The next thing, they were trying to take my clothes off; finding this stoutly resisted, they turned up my sleeves to the shoulders. Their taste differed from mine, for, while I was thinking what a cold, ugly colour a white arm looked beside their warm, brown ones, they were crying out in admiration. One woman kissed my feet (the island kiss) and sniffed softly up and down my arms. She was plainly saying to the others, 'She's just like a pickaninny; I would like to have her for a pet,' holding out her arms as she spoke and going through the motions of tossing and caressing a baby. My hands and feet were measured by theirs and found to be much smaller (they were large women made on a more generous scale than I). 'Pickaninny hands and feet,' they said. The discovery of vaccination marks caused great excitement. In a moment all their husbands' heads appeared at the doors and windows. My sleeves, in spite of my struggles, were dragged to my shoulders and, to my dismay, my petticoats were whipped up to my knees. At that I began to cry, when the men instantly disappeared, and except for an occasional sniffing the women behaved with more decorum. One woman was most anxious that I should stop on the island with her. I really think she had some hope that she might keep me as a sort of pet monkey. At last they were warned that the ship would be off soon, so they fled to their canoes. . . .

In the afternoon Louis was dictating to Lloyd who used his typewriter. All the air and most of the room was cut off from them by heads at the portholes. I watched the faces and saw one intelligent old man explaining to the others that Lloyd was playing an accompaniment to Louis singing; the old man several times tried to follow the tune but found it impossible. He did not appear to think it a good song, and once, with difficulty, restrained his laughter.

13th. — Tom Day is — must be — 'the flower of the Pacific'. Tom is fifty years of age with a strong, alert figure and the mobile face of an actor; his eyes are blue-grey in deep orbits, blazing with energy and drink and high spirits. 'Tom Day' is not his real name, he says, and Tom Drunk would do quite as well; he had found it necessary to go to the expense of a shilling to have it changed, as he had three times deserted from men-of-war. 'I've been in prison for it,' he said cheerfully, 'and I got the cat for it, and if you like you can see the stars and stripes on my back yet.' He took pleasure in representing himself as the most desperate of ruffians. Tin Jack asked him to go back to Sydney with him. 'I couldn't leave my old woman behind,' said he, 'and besides, you see, I got into trouble there. The fact is, I've got another wife there, and I think I'd do better to keep away.'

(*Tin Jack came to a bad end. He possessed a certain fixed income which, however, was not large enough for Jack's liking, so he spent most of the year as a South Seas trader, using the whole of his year's income in one wild burst of dissipation in the town of Sydney. One of his favourite amusements was to hire a hansom cab for the day, put the driver inside, and drive the vehicle himself, calling upon various passers-by to join him at the nearest public house. Some years ago, when Jack was at his station, he received word that his trustee, who was in charge of his property, had levanted with it all. Whereupon poor Jack put a pistol to his head and blew out what brains he possessed. He was a beautiful creature, terribly annoying at times, but with something childlike and appealing — I think he was close to what the Scotch call a natural — that made one forgive pranks in him that would be unforgivable in others. He was very proud of being the original of 'Tommy Hadden' in *The Wrecker* and carried the book wherever he went.)

Tom Day

Letter to E. L. Burlingame
S.S. Janet Nicoll, *off Peru Island, Kingsmills Group*
July 13, 1890

. . . I shall probably return to Samoa direct, having given up all idea of returning to civilisation in the meanwhile. There, on my ancestral acres which I purchased six months ago from a blind Scots blacksmith, you will please address me until further notice. The name of the ancestral acres is going to be Vailima; . . . (they) run to upwards of three hundred; they enjoy the ministrations of five streams, hence the name. They are all at the present moment under a trackless covering of magnificent forest, which would be worth a great deal if it grew beside a railway terminus. To me, as it stands, it represents a handsome deficit. Obliging natives from the cannibal islands are now cutting it down at my expense. You would be able to run your magazine to much greater advantage if the terms of the authors were on the same scale with those of my cannibals. We also have a house about the size of a manufacturer's lodge. 'Tis but the egg of the future palace, over the details of which on paper Mrs Stevenson and I have already shed real tears; what it will be when it comes to paying for it, I leave to you to imagine. . . .

R.L.S.

The Vailima Household: L. to R: Joe Strong, Margaret Stevenson,
Lloyd Osbourne, Louis and in front of Fanny, Belle Strong and son Austin

With Vailima servants

My dear Charles, — I have stayed here a week while Lloyd and my wife continue to voyage in the *Janet Nicoll*; this I did partly to see the convict system, partly to shorten my stay in the extreme cold — hear me with my extreme! *moi qui suis originaire d'Edinbourg* — of Sydney at this season. I am feeling very seedy, utterly fatigued, and overborne with sleep. I have a fine old gentleman of a doctor, who attends and cheers and entertains, if he does not cure me; but even with his ministrations I am almost incapable of the exertion sufficient for this letter; and I am really, as I write, falling down with sleep. What is necessary to say, I must try to say shortly. Lloyd goes to clear out our establishments: pray keep him in funds, if I have any; if I have not, pray try to raise them. . . . Here is the idea: to install ourselves, at the risk of bankruptcy, in Samoa. It is not the least likely it will pay (although it may); but it is almost certain it will support life, with very few external expenses. If I die, it will be an endowment for the survivors, at least for my wife and Lloyd; and my mother, who might prefer to go home, has her own. Hence I believe I shall do well to hurry my installation. The letters are already in

Visiting warship at Vailima

part done; in part done is a novel for Scribner; in the course of the next twelve months I should receive a considerable amount of money. . . . Better to build the house and have a roof and farm of my own; and thereafter, with a livelihood assured, save and prepay. There is my livelihood, all but books and wine, ready in a nutshell; and it ought to be more easy to save and repay afterwards. Excellent, say you, but will you save and will you repay? I do not know, said the Bell of Old Bow. . . . The deuce of the affair is that I do not know when I shall see you and Colvin. I guess you will have to come and see me: many a time already we have arranged the details of your visit in the yet unbuilt house on the mountain. I shall be able to get a decent wine from Noumea. We shall be able to give you a decent welcome, and talk of old days. . . .

The morrow. — I feel better, but still dim and groggy. Tonight I go to the governor's; such a lark — no dress clothes — twenty-four hours' notice — able-bodied Polish tailor — suit made for a man with the figure of a puncheon — same hastily altered for self with the figure of a bodkin — sight inconceivable. Never mind; dress clothes, 'which nobody can deny'; and the officials have been all so civil that I liked neither to refuse nor to appear in mufti. Bad dress clothes only prove you are a grisly ass; no dress clothes, even when explained, indicate a want of respect. . . .

View of Noumea harbour

Penal Settlement, Noumea

I hope you never forget to remember me to your father, who has always a place in my heart, as I hope I have a little in his. His kindness helped me infinitely when you and I were young; I recall it with gratitude and affection in this town of convicts at the world's end. There are very few things, my dear Charles, worth mention: on a retrospect of life, the day's flash and colour, one day with another, flames, dazzles, and puts to sleep; and when the days are gone, like a fast-flying thaumatrope, they make but a single pattern. Only a few things stand out; and among these — most plainly to me — Rutland Square. — Ever, my dear Charles, your affectionate friend,

R.L.S.

P.S. — Just returned from trying on the dress clothes. Lord, you should see the coat! It stands out at the waist like a bustle, the flaps across in front, the sleeves are like bags.

184

Letter to Henry James
Union Club, Sydney, August 1890

. . . I must tell you plainly — I can't tell Colvin — I do not think I shall come to England more than once, and then it'll be to die. Health I enjoy in the tropics; even here, which they call sub- or semi-tropics, I come only to catch cold. I have not been out since my arrival; live here in a nice bedroom by the fireside, and read books and letters from Henry James. . . . But I can't go out. The thermometer was nearly down to 50 degrees the other day — no temperature for me, Mr James: how should I do in England? I fear not at all. Am I very sorry? I am sorry about seven or eight people in England, and one or two in the States. And outside of that, I simply prefer Samoa. These are the words of honesty and soberness. (I am fasting from all but sin, coughing . . . a couple of eggs and a cup of tea.) I was never fond of towns, houses, society or (it seems) civilisation. Nor yet it seems was I ever fond of (what is technically called) God's green earth. The sea, islands, the islanders, the island life and climate, make and keep me truly happier. These last two years I have been much at sea, and I have never wearied; sometimes I have indeed grown impatient for some destination; more often I was sorry that the voyage drew so early to an end; and never once did I lose my fidelity to blue water and a ship. It is plain, then, that for me my exile to the place of schooners and islands can be in no sense regarded as a calamity. Goodbye just now . . . I must take a turn at my proofs.

R.L.S.

Main Street, Noumea

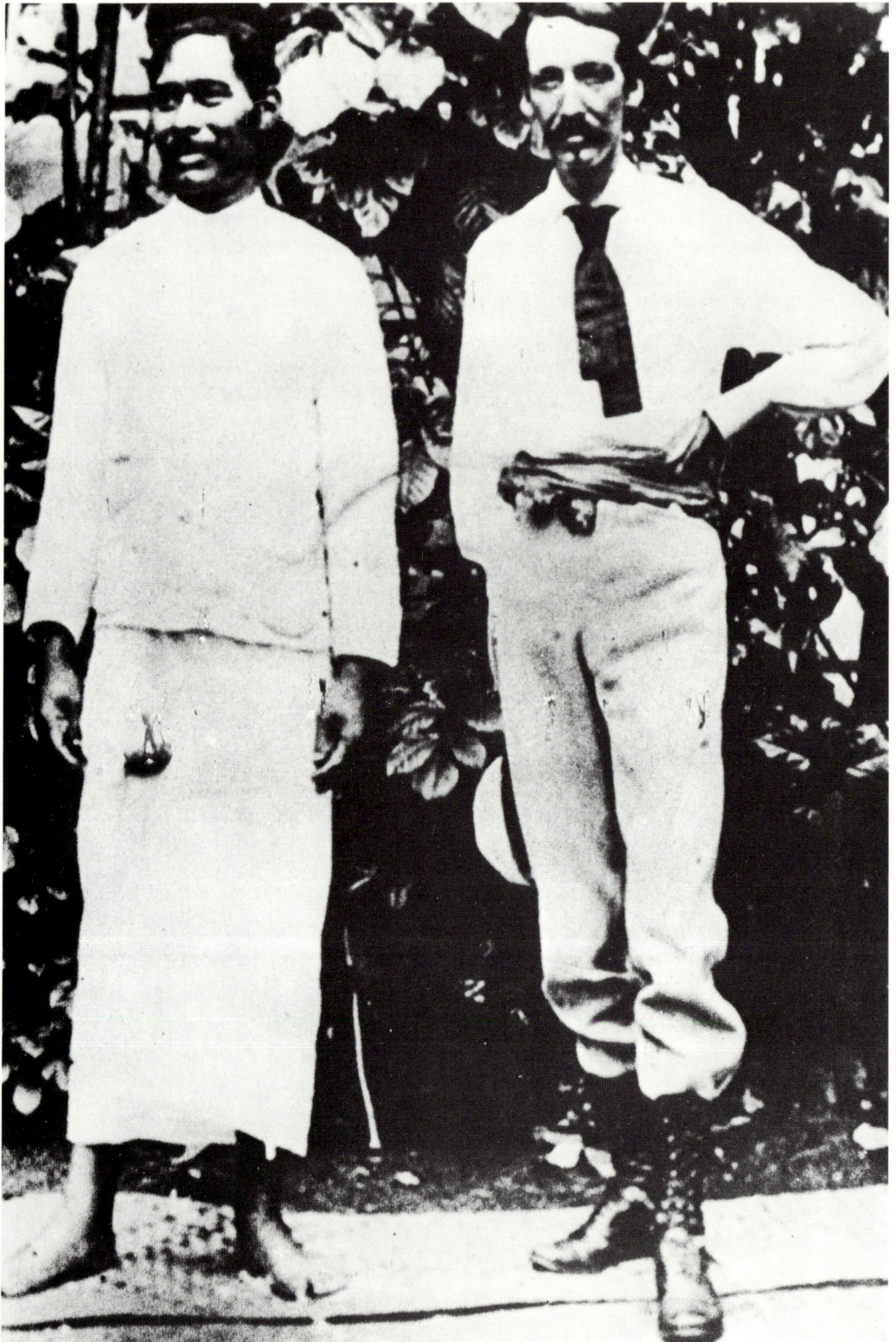

The last photograph, Vailima 1894

Letter to Mrs Charles Fairchild
Union Club, Sydney, September 1890

My dear Mrs Fairchild, — . . . It is always harshness that one regrets . . . I regret also my letter to Dr Hyde. Yes, I do; . . . it was virtuous to defend Damien; but it was harsh to strike so hard at Dr Hyde. When I wrote the letter, I believed he would bring an action, in which case I knew I could be beggared. And as yet there has come no action; the injured Doctor has contented himself up to now with the (truly innocuous) vengeance of calling me a 'Bohemian Crank', and I have deeply wounded one of his colleagues whom I esteemed and liked.

Well, such is life. You are quite right; our civilisation is a hollow fraud — all the fun of life is lost by it; all it gains is that a larger number of persons can continue to be contemporaneously unhappy on the surface of the globe. . . . When, observe that word, which I will write again and larger — WHEN you come to see us in Samoa, you will see for yourself a healthy and happy people.

You see, you are one of the very few of our friends rich enough to come and see us; and when my house is built, and the road is made, and we have enough fruit planted and poultry and pigs raised, it is undeniable that you must come — must is the word; that is the way in which I speak to ladies. You and Fairchild — we'll arrange details in good time. It will be the salvation of your soul, and make you willing to die.

Let me tell you this: in '74 or 5 there came to stay with my father and mother a certain Mr Seed, a prime minister or something of New Zealand [he was Servant to the Customs and Marine Department]. He spotted what my complaint was; told me that I had no business to stay in Europe; that I should find all I cared for, and all that was good for me, in the Navigator Islands; sat up till four in the morning persuading me, demolishing my scruples. And I resisted: I refused to go so far from my father and mother. O, it was virtuous, and O, wasn't it silly! But my father, who was always my dearest, got to his grave without that pang; and now in 1890, I (or what is left of me) go at last to the Navigator Islands. God go with us! It is but a Pisgah sight when all is said; I go there only to grow old and die; but when you come, you will see it is a fair place for the purpose.

ROBERT LOUIS STEVENSON

The empty hall at Vailima

APPENDIX 1:

This excerpt from the marriage certificate of Robert Louis Stevenson and Fanny Osbourne is interesting for its curious mis-spellings and also the fact that Fanny described herself not as 'divorced' but as 'widowed'. The minister was Rev. Dr William A. Scott, of St John's Presbyterian Church in San Francisco, and president of the local St Andrew's Society. The couple exchanged silver rings since Stevenson could not afford the more traditional gold wedding rings and Rev. Scott received for his services ten dollars and a copy of *Christianity Confirmed by Jewish and Heathen Testimony* by Thomas Stevenson.

APPENDIX 2:

This map of *Treasure Island*, frontispiece of the first edition published by Cassell & Co in 1883, is not, sadly, the original drawn by Lloyd Osbourne in Braemar which inspired the book's creation as *The Sea Cook*, a serial for *Young Folk's Magazine*.

'The proofs came' (from Cassell) wrote Stevenson, 'they were corrected, but I heard nothing of the map. I wrote and asked: was told it had never been received, and sat aghast. It is one thing to draw a map at random and write up a story to the measurements. It is quite another to have to design a map to suit the data. I did it, and the map was drawn again in my father's office, with embellishments of blowing whales and sailing ships. But somehow it was never *Treasure Island* to me'.

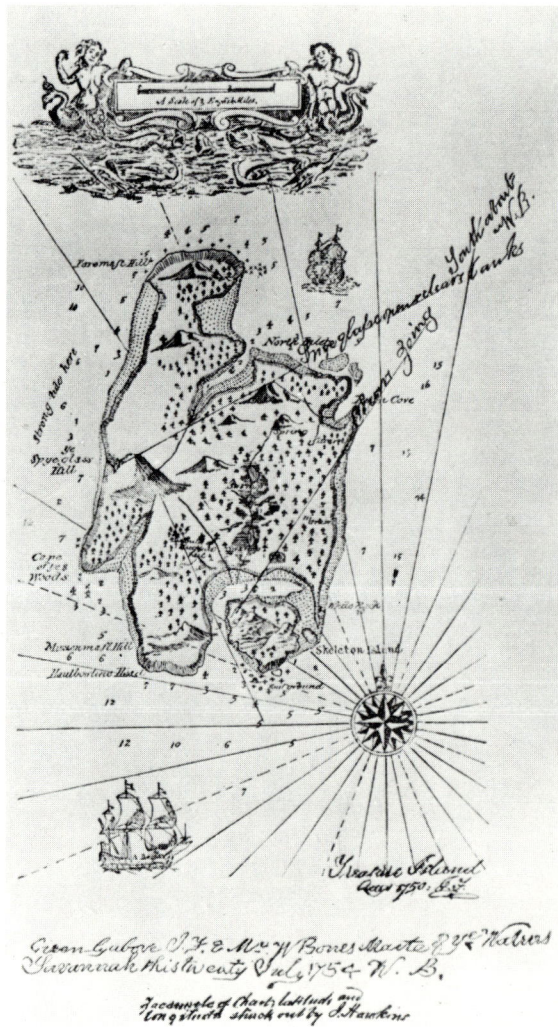

APPENDIX 3:

A sea- and travel-stained page from Stevenson's journal relating to his travels around the Kona coast of the Island of Hawaii, for Saturday, 27 April 1889.

THE STAINED JOURNAL OF STEVENSON'S TRAVELS AROUND THE KONA COAST OF THE ISLAND OF HAWAII BEGINS ON SATURDAY, APRIL 27, 1889.

Page from the manuscript of *Weir of Hermiston*. Stevenson was at work on this novel on the morning of his death at Vailima, 3 December 1894.

cried in a choked voice.

38

miss me?" He battled—

The doctor turned about and looked him all over with a clinical eye. The young man's whole attitude smelt of domestic discord; a far more stupid man than Dr. Gregory must have divined the truth; but ninety-nine men out of a hundred, even if they had been equally inclined to charity, would have blundered by some touch of charitable exaggeration. The doctor was better inspired. After a moment's pause, he told the truth—

"Well, I'll tell you why," said he— "It was when you had the measles, Mr. Archibald, you had them gey and ill; and I thought myself you were going to slip between my fingers. The day came when there was a change, and I went down to announce it to your father. 'There is a change, Hermiston,' said I. He said nothing, but glowered at me (if you'll excuse me) like a wild beast. 'A change for the better,' said I. Well, I heard him take his breath—"

And the doctor, leaving no opportunity for any anticlimax, made his escape.